Flower Arranging
1961-62.
less Cutters-
Available Company T.L.
1961 · 1962

The Art of Flower
and Foliage Arrangement

*To members of my family,
all ardent gardeners*

The Art of Flower and Foliage Arrangement

ANNA HONG RUTT

Formerly Head of the Art Department
Northwestern University, Evanston, Illinois

All flower arrangements by
ANNA HONG RUTT

All photographs by
ELEMORE MORGAN

New York 1960   THE MACMILLAN COMPANY

Fourth Printing, 1960

Printed in the United States of America

Library of Congress catalog card number: 58-5464

Foreword

The arranging of flowers and foliage has come to be one of the most widely practiced of the visual arts. Especially in the United States has this subject had appeal for beauty-conscious people of all ages. Classes in arrangement are given in college departments of art, landscape design, forestry, horticulture, and home economics, as well as in some high and elementary schools. Members of garden clubs are serious students of the art of flower arrangement.

Because there are established principles and elements to understand, those who practice flower arrangement first need to study. This book, which has been written as a guide for them, attempts not only to help beginners but also to enlarge the understanding of advanced practitioners.

In the first few chapters the fundamentals of design in flower arrangement are presented and the vocabulary used in this art is explained. In the remainder of the book these fundamentals are applied in the design of arrangements of various kinds for many different purposes.

The principles and elements of art are not just for artists and judges to use; they are for everyone. They provide the key that unlocks the door to understanding why any example of creative art is ugly or beautiful.

Contents

CONTENTS

PART I

The Art Principles

The study of flower arrangement may be approached in several ways. In teaching college classes the author has found it most effective to base the subject on the principles and the elements of art. These are the same principles and elements that are used in all space arts.

In studying objects that have been considered beautiful through the centuries, experts in esthetics have been able to determine what qualities are common to all of them. From these observations it is generally agreed that good proportion, balance, dominance, and rhythm are present in all man-made things that have beauty. These qualities are called the major principles of art (or design).

The minor art principles, which sometimes overlap the major principles, are less clearly defined. Those that apply most to flower arrangement are transition, repetition, radiation, variation, and contrast.

The art principles are basic in the creation of beauty. They should not be regarded as mere rules; they are the rocks underneath the changing tides of fashion, experimentation, and new materials.

Apply these Art or Design Principles	To these Art Elements	To attain these Objectives
Proportion	Line	Beauty
Balance	Form	Expressiveness
Dominance	Pattern	Suitability
Rhythm	Texture	
	Color	

Chapter 1

PROPORTION

Proportion is the art principle that underlies all the other principles. Good proportion means *pleasing relationship in size and shape* among things or parts of things.

Mankind has found somewhat different proportions pleasing in different lands and at different times; however there is a surprising similarity everywhere in proportions that are considered to be beautiful.

Classical Proportions. These were established by the ancient Greeks and are used as models even today. The Greeks formulated rules of beautiful proportions that were based on the human body. As their culture changed, their choice of proportions gradually changed from the sturdy, broad columns of the Doric order to the final weaker, more slender, and more elaborate columns of the Corinthian order. The book *Dynamic Symmetry* by Hambidge presents a study of classical proportions and their relation to certain mathematical measurements.

Knowledge of some of the precise proportions used by the ancients can be useful to advanced flower arrangers as well as to other artists. The following diagram shows how to find the most pleasing dividing point on any line and how to find the correct measurements for a rectangular oblong that has the beautiful proportions of the *golden section of Euclid*. These measurements may be used in designing flower arrangements.

The following explanation is taken from the author's earlier book, *Home Furnishing;* however, it can also be found in elementary

2

geometry books. Start with any straight line, possibly the same as the length of a low container, or the height of a complete flower arrangement. With the length of the line AD as the diameter, draw a circle tangent to the line AD at the point D. Suppose that the point E is the center of the circle. Now draw a line connecting A and E, establishing the point F where the line AE crosses the circle. With AF as radius draw a second circle with A as center, intersecting AD at G. *The point G is the mean division point of the line AD; it is the most harmonic division point on this line.* GD : AG : : AG : AD.

PROPORTION

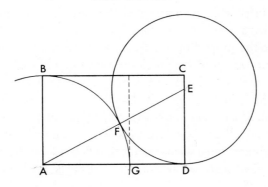

Using the same diagram, a rectangular oblong having the proportions of the golden section of Euclid can be easily constructed. Erect a perpendicular line upward from A; where it crosses the circle you will locate the point B. The line AB is the dimension required to form the *oblong ABCD, which is the golden section.* Erect a perpendicular at G, thus forming a square area and a smaller area. The smaller area is to the square as the square is to the whole area, which is a requirement of the golden oblong. This oblong may be vertical or horizontal; its beautiful proportions may be used in making a niche or a flower arrangement.

Proportion in Japanese Flower Arrangements. Japanese flower arrangers in general favor approximately the same proportions that the Greeks used. In the traditional Japanese classical arrangement the plant material is about one and one-half times as tall as the container. In other words, the plant material is three-fifths of the total height and the container is two-fifths. Slender tips are not counted in these dimensions. Although the proportions vary slightly in different schools, the secondary line of the design, representing Man, is usually about two-thirds of the primary line (Heaven) and the tertiary line (Earth) is about one-third of the primary line. When the natural characteristics of the plant materials being used are contrary to these proportions, Japanese arrangers often select whatever proportions are fitting regardless of traditions (see page 131).

Proportion in American Flower Arrangements. American flower arrangers, in general, have accepted the basic ideas of good proportion that have developed in both East and West. In their homes, they adapt the proportions of flower arrangements to suit the wall areas behind them and the articles of furniture on which they stand. In American flower shows one generally accepted idea is that the plant materials in arrangements should be *at least one and one-half times* as tall as a medium or tall container, and *at least one and one-half times* as tall as the width of a low container. The maximum dimension is not stated, however, for that depends on the *background space*, the *plant material*, and *theme*, and finally on the *taste* of the arranger.

Examples of poor proportions:
   Equal heights in container and plant materials
   Equal width and equal height in total arrangement
   Equal height of container and figurines
   A niche arrangement filling half of the space or less in height, in width, or in total volume
Examples of good proportions:
   Plant materials that are one and one-half times or more as high as a tall container
   Plant materials that are three times as wide as a low container
   An upright S design with two-thirds of the plant materials above the rim of the container

A low, flat arrangement with only two-thirds of the water surface covered by the plant materials

The proportions of the wall area before which an arrangement stands affect its dimensions. A tall, narrow space may suggest an arrangement that is four times as tall as a tall container. Such an arrangement, however, should be very thin at the top. A low broad space such as between the television set and a picture hung above it can accommodate only a horizontal arrangement.

A strong *base* also permits arrangements to be taller than usual; arrangements that stand on the floor may reach almost to the ceiling, if they look stable.

Containers that are dark in color or strong in construction material can support much larger arrangements than others. The *weight* of the plant material affects proportions too; airy plants may extend much higher than heavy ones.

Scale. *Scale* refers to relative *sizes* only, not to shapes. In flower arrangement scale has many applications, some of which are:

1. Relation of the size of an arrangement to the *room* wherein it stands. A large room takes a large arrangement, and so on.
2. Relation of the size of an arrangement to its *placement:* a table, shelf, pedestal, or niche. For example, a coffee table arrangement is usually small and low.
3. Relation of the size of the *container* to the *plant materials.* There should usually be more plant material than container. In an arrangement no flower should be more than one-third the size of the container, in the work of beginners, especially.
4. Relation of the size of the *plant materials* to *one another.* Very tiny flowers do not look well with very large ones, such as lilies-of-the-valley with calla-lilies.
5. Relation of size of the *accessories* to the *rest of the composition.* The accessories should be consistent in size. They are often too small to be effective (see page 100).

PROBLEMS IN PROPORTION
(Suggestions from which to choose)
(Read Chapter 20)

1. Draw in outline a page of containers of various sizes and shapes, including tall, medium, low, broad, and narrow, with and without bases. Draw a group of lines extending from the top of each container to show how high and how wide the plant materials may be in an arrangement. It is not necessary to draw leaves or flowers.
2. Make a tall, narrow foliage arrangement suitable for a tall, narrow space. For height use long leaves like iris, sansevieria, or aspidistra, or other spike materials such as dock, cattails, or sections of cornstalks or bamboo. Just above the rim of the container add some twigs with broader leaves like oak, poplar, loquat, magnolia, or viburnum. If a quart milk bottle must be used for a container, it can be set inside a roll of brown or leaf-green paper.
3. Start a scrapbook for pictures of flower arrangements.

A THEME ARRANGEMENT, entitled "Wake Up." The proportions of this triangular composition are satisfactory, for the height is about one and a half times the width, and the cane and the bundle of rice straw are in scale with the large rooster. The rhythm is outstanding, the large curves in rice and cane repeating the curves of the rooster's tail and breast.

A STYLIZED HORIZONTAL ARRANGEMENT of amaryllis is suitable for a dinner table or the top of a cabinet. The proportion here is good, since the height is one third of the total width.

This **NATURAL ARRANGEMENT** of somewhat triangular form is in strong contrast with the stylized arrangement above. Its proportion is pleasing, because the plant material is almost twice the width of the container. The magnolia blossom and buds form an inner triangle.

Chapter 2

BALANCE

The second art principle that flower arrangers must study is *balance*. In flower arrangement balance means stability, actual and visual. Not only must an arrangement *be* balanced so that it will not upset, but it must also *look* well balanced. Balance implies repose and steadiness. To obtain balance means to produce equilibrium by arranging objects on both sides of a central vertical axis so that the opposing forces neutralize one another. Nearly everyone has a fair sense of material balance and through practice becomes sensitive to fine adjustments in balance. Two kinds of balance, *symmetrical* and *asymmetrical*, are used in flower arrangement as in all the arts.

Occidental art and architecture are based on *symmetrical balance*. This kind of balance is our heritage from classical Greek and Roman art forms, and is the basis of all traditional decorative period styles of the West.

Oriental art is based on *asymmetrical balance*. From the Japanese and Chinese we have learned much about asymmetrical or informal balance in painting, landscape design, and flower arrangement. Some Oriental teachers believe that the seemingly vacant side of a painting or flower arrangement is a place for the play of the observer's imagination and for meditation and rest. They say that the empty space on one side in a design is for you, the observer, to enter into, so that you also may have a part in making this picture, whether it is a painting or a flower arrangement. Such ideas help us to realize the spiritual significance of the arts.

Symmetrical or Formal Balance. In a flower arrangement symmetrical or bisymmetrical balance usually means that the weight and appearance of the plant materials are about the same on both sides of an imaginary vertical axis rising from the center of a symmetrical container and base. While this kind of balance is restful, stately, and dignified, it is also rather static and is sometimes dull and unimaginative (see pages 13, 23, 102).

When used, symmetrical balance should usually be carried out completely. That is, a symmetrical arrangement should never have just one accessory at one side of it, instead there might be a pair, with one on each side, equidistant from the center, or one accessory in the center. The center of interest in a symmetrical arrangement may be diagonal or otherwise asymmetrical in pattern, without disturbing the symmetrical effect. A symmetrical arrangement should not be placed against an asymmetrical background.

Asymmetrical or Informal Balance. Asymmetrical balance in flower arrangement means that the plant material is *not similarly arranged* on both sides of an imaginary vertical axis through the center of the container. The two sides may or may not have equal amounts of plant materials. Asymmetrical balance is subtle, creative, emotional, and stimulating. Although more difficult to achieve, it is apt to be more personally satisfying than formal balance.

Frequently in asymmetrical balance the solid plant material masses do not appear to balance one another, therefore it is necessary to regard *the voids* as significant enough to balance *the solids*. This is puzzling for some American flower arrangers to understand or to explain. Nevertheless most of them eventually find that they prefer this occult balance of spaces to the more obvious symmetrical balance. Asymmetrical balance is, in fact, sometimes spoken of as *occult balance*.

Asymmetrical arrangements may be balanced in several different ways: *self-balanced, balanced by placement, or balanced by accessories.*

Self-balance is usually the most satisfactory kind of balance to employ in a flower arrangement. In asymmetrical self-balanced arrangements the lines and masses are so distributed on both sides of a central vertical axis through the center of the container that although opposing sides are distinctly different in shape, they have the same total visual weight, so that the result is in equilibrium. The lazy S, the upright semicircle, and some verticals are examples of this kind of balance (see page 150). The famous Japanese three-point classical design usually has self-balance, also known as self-contained balance.

Balance by placement means that an arrangement is *not balanced in itself*, but is heavier on one side of the container than on the other, however it appears balanced when placed in the right relation to its base or its setting (see page 13). Arrangements that are balanced by placement are often pleasing and subtle, but they are the subject of controversy too. Some designers maintain that arrangements that are heavier on one side than on the other have imbalance that cannot be remedied merely by placement.

In arrangements that are balanced by placement not only is the stem holder placed off-center in the container, but the container stands off-center on its base, which in turn is also placed slightly off-center in a niche or on a table or shelf.

An arranger should learn to locate the *imaginary vertical axis* in an arrangement that is balanced by placement and should mentally complete the rectangle which the axis divides. The amount of solids and voids on each side of the axis may be easily compared in this way. In time a thoughtful designer learns to evaluate the balance of materials against empty spaces.

In an L-*shaped arrangement* the imaginary vertical axis is a little to the right of the upright line. In a *right-angled triangle* that faces the same way as a letter L, the imaginary vertical axis is also to the right of the tallest line, which is usually directly over the stem holder.

In a *pitcher arrangement* the balance depends upon the design of the flower arrangement. Some designers prefer to follow the thought for which the pitcher was intended, and let the plant materials pour over the lip, with the center of interest near the handle. The highest point is usually located over the center of interest, so that the vertical axis passes through both of them. Other designers use a tall pitcher as an ordinary vase and make in it a tall asymmetrical arrangement, with the vertical axis slightly off-center toward the handle (see page 238).

Balance by accessories means that an asymmetrical arrangement may acquire the balance that it lacks by the addition of one or more accessories that are separate from the arrangement. These accessories may be anything from a figurine to a few leaves in an ash tray. The accessory may be placed on the strong or the weak side of the arrangement, but is usually located on the side that has the least weight in plant materials.

A *combination* of symmetrical and asymmetrical balance in one arrangement may cause difficulties. For an asymmetrical arrangement the container should not have two handles, because the two handles stress symmetry. Likewise an asymmetrical container like a pitcher, gravy boat, or a free form of any kind should not hold a symmetrical arrangement. An off-center arrangement does not look well when placed at the center of a symmetrical background space.

Weight. The *apparent visual weight* and the *actual weight* of plant materials are basic factors in balance in flower arrangement. The *visual weight* of plant materials *increases:*

1. the farther the materials are from the central axis
2. the higher they are in the composition
3. the more compact they are
4. the stronger they are in color intensity
5. the darker they are in color value
6. the warmer they are in hue

Some *guides in elementary balance* in flower arrangements are:

1. Use containers that are as dark as the flowers or leaves.
2. Keep dark colors low in arrangements.
3. Locate the tip of the tallest line over the base of that same line.
4. Make the two sides seem about equally heavy.
5. Make the chief vertical area fairly compact.
6. Make the lowest part of the arrangement the most compact.
7. Keep the center of interest low and on or near the vertical axis.
8. Place the largest flowers at the center of interest.

BALANCE

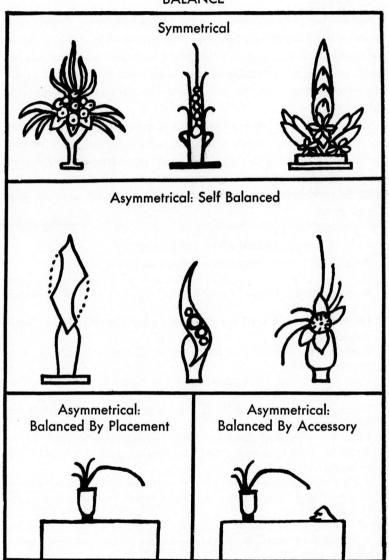

Symmetrical

Asymmetrical: Self Balanced

Asymmetrical:
Balanced By Placement

Asymmetrical:
Balanced By Accessory

13

9. Use only small forms for top and for edges of arrangements.
10. Correct a top-heavy arrangement by placing a base beneath the container.

Nature should be our teacher with regard to balance. Perfect symmetry is not natural in plant life, although healthy growing things are usually well balanced. An elm tree or a locust is an excellent example of asymmetrical balance often with voids to counter the solid masses of foliage. The fir tree represents symmetrical balance in nature.

Strongly lopsided compositions do not reflect nature. A large, tall container holding a top-heavy, long branch at one side could be kept upright by filling it with rocks, but visual equilibrium would be lost because the observer would be uneasy about it. Common sense is a guide to good balance in flower arrangement as well as in all other things in life.

PROBLEMS IN BALANCE
(Suggestions from which to choose)

1. Draw a seesaw balanced by two blocks of equal weight (*bisymmetrical* or *symmetrical*);
   Draw a seesaw with a large block balancing a smaller block (*asymmetrical*);
   Draw a scale balancing a small weight against a bundle of straw (*asymmetrical*).
2. Draw a heavy line for a mantel shelf. On it draw a container holding sticks and a separate sphere for *balance by accessory*.
3. Make an arrangement of three, five, or seven sticks illustrating any kind of balance.
4. Make a *symmetrical flower or foliage arrangement* to place in the middle of a table, shelf, or desk. A container with two handles may be used (see page 239).
5. Make a *self-balanced asymmetrical arrangement* in a container without handles. (Same weight on both sides of center but different in shape (see page 84).
6. Make a *lopsided arrangement* that is off-center in a low container but is balanced by standing off-center on a long base, table, or window sill (see page 237).

AN ASYMMETRICAL ARRANGEMENT, BALANCED BY PLACEMENT

AN ASYMMETRICAL ARRANGEMENT WITH SELF BALANCE

SYMMETRICAL BALANCE is suitable for a church arrangement or for any formal occasion. The stock is white, lavender, and violet, the calla-lilies are white, and the container is gray, making a monochromatic color scheme.

Chapter 3

DOMINANCE (EMPHASIS)

Dominance or _emphasis_ is one of the major art principles; it is very important in flower arrangement, for dominance helps to produce _unity_. That is, by emphasis on one thing and subordination of others, competition is removed and cohesion is made possible. If a flower arrangement contains two or more equal attractions, they will pull the design apart. Any one of the following kinds of dominance will help to hold a design together.

Dominant Idea. A dominant idea or theme is advisable in a flower arrangement. One idea may be expressed so forcibly by all the plant materials and the container and base that no conflicting idea can exist. The line, form, texture, and color may be chosen so as to express this dominant idea. This aspect of flower arrangement helps to make it a fine art.

Dominant Movement. The emphasis must be chiefly on one kind of movement in order to have rhythm in an arrangement or a picture. A rhythm of curves is the most common movement in flower arrangement, sometimes accompanied by a minor rhythm of radiating or diagonal lines or a combination of lines.

Dominant Direction. Positive emphasis on one direction is necessary for dynamic rhythm, even though some minor lines go in another direction. The effect is static when equal lines go in opposite directions.

Dominant Line. In nearly all line arrangements, a dominant line is evident. It is usually accompanied by related lines, and sometimes by some lesser opposing lines. A dominating line or linear

17

pattern is also present in many line-mass and mass arrangements.

Dominant Mass. In a good mass arrangement, as in a good building, there is a dominant mass. It is the main body of a mass arrangement, in which the focal area is located. The remainder of the arrangement is smaller, less solid, and less important.

Dominant Texture. Strong dominance of one kind of texture is advisable in most arrangements so that unity in texture results. For example, the delicate textures dominate in a combination of sweet peas, roses, nandina foliage, glass container, and a lace doily. The roses and nandina foliage are somewhat more sturdy, but are friendly to the other textures. Even when texture contrast is deliberately sought, one kind of texture should dominate.

Dominant Color. Dominance of *either warmth* or *coolness* in the colors of a flower arrangement is an elementary requirement. Dominance of *one chosen hue* is also necessary for beauty; an arrangement that is half red and half green has unpleasant competition within itself. Dominance of either light or medium *values* is usually desirable in flower arrangements. Harmony calls for the dominance of *intensity* in one color only; for example, bright blue and bright vermilion make a crude combination, even when they are unequal in quantity.

Dominant Flowers. In a mixed mass bouquet one kind of flower should dominate in quantity. Without this dominance interest is divided, scattered, and quickly lost. In most arrangements the flowers used for a focal point dominate because of their size and color, although it is quite possible for the secondary spike or stem screen to dominate in quantity. Equal quantities of different kinds of flowers are undesirable.

Dominant Area: the Center of Interest. A landscaped garden, a living room, or a painting should have a center of interest, a place that attracts the attention first and last and holds it longest. Likewise, any planned flower arrangement should usually have a center of interest although it may be obscure in some cases. Within the area of the center of interest there may be a particular point that demands more attention than its surroundings; this may be called the focal point. The center of interest is usually located near the place where all the stems of the plant materials converge, because the attention is naturally drawn there.

The chief function of the center of interest is to draw together all the separate parts of a design, providing a place on which to focus the attention. This is the heart or core of the flower arrangement.

Ways and means of creating *a center of interest* in a flower arrangement:

1. Concentrate the flowers at the area selected. Even with only one kind of flower in the entire arrangement this is a requirement.
2. Place the largest flowers there. This is possible whether you have one or more kinds of flowers.
3. Use roundish flowers there because round and oval shapes attract and hold the attention better than spikes or trumpets.
4. Place your most beautiful or interesting flowers there.
5. Place the brightest flowers there.
6. Secure the strongest value contrast there. If the focal area is lacking in interest, add something light and an edge of something dark.
7. Provide some plain planes nearby. Below or beside the area of interest place some large leaves which will allow attention to focus on the center of interest.
8. Have density around the focal point except in sparse line arrangements. Looking through stems and through the arrangement near the focal point detracts from its effect.
9. Bring all converging lines of the composition to the center of interest. The more converging lines there are, the stronger the center of interest should be.
10. Subordinate the rivals of the focal material; choose only one queen for the picture.

The *location* of the center of interest can be best determined by experimentation and thoughtful consideration. Some designers maintain that you can locate the correct focal center by diagonal lines drawn from the tips of all spikes on each side of the arrangement to the container or table on the opposite side of the arrangement. The place where most of these lines cross the vertical axis is said to be the focal center; the center of interest should be located there or nearby.

The *art principles* are useful in locating the center of interest. Balance, proportion, rhythm, and dominance enter into it.

Balance requires that the center of interest be in the lower half of the total composition, so that the arrangement will not be top-heavy; however, it should not be so low that it appears to be sagging down. It should usually be near the vertical axis for side-to-side balance.

Good proportion restricts us from placing the center of interest in the exact center of the composition, horizontally, unless the arrangement is exactly bisymmetrical.

Rhythm (see Chapter 4) guides us in the location of the center of interest in an arrangement. For example, in a right-angled triangular flower arrangement the center of interest must be placed at or near the hub, where the stem holder is located, because all the radiating stem lines carry the eye to that place. Some arrangers say that the focal area should be located at the foot of the tallest line because your eye is led to that spot. In general in any kind of arrangement the center of interest is located at the approximate intersection of the main lines of the linear pattern.

The *shape* of the focal area may repeat the shape of the entire arrangement, as a triangle within a triangle. The established design is strengthened by this repetition.

The *strength* of the center of interest should be determined by the type and location of the arrangement. Some modern arrangements look well with a strong center of interest. The bull's-eye or target effect, however, is not in favor now. A very strong focal area too often appears to be unnatural and insensitive. Three bold round flowers used as a focal area are usually too trite to be interesting.

A subtle center of interest is desirable in many arrangements. All natural arrangements, whether line or mass, should have very little emphasis at the focal area.

Plant materials rather than containers should dominate in a flower arrangement. Containers should therefore usually be plain. Fashions change and decorated containers may be temporarily popular, but that does not make them generally acceptable by people with trained taste.

Figurines and other *accessories* should be subordinate to plant materials when shown in flower shows, unless the schedule states otherwise. For home use a beautiful figurine may well be the dominant factor in a composition, because there the plant materials do not need the emphasis that they should have in a flower show.

PROBLEMS IN DOMINANCE
(Suggestions from which to choose)

1. Draw a heavy line for a tray. Off-center on the tray draw the outlines of a *vegetable arrangement*, consisting of an eggplant, with some turnips touching it and some okra next to the turnips. The eggplant is the focal area because of its size.
2. Make an arrangement of *one kind of flower* and any foliage. Make a concentration of the flowers near the rim of the container for a focal area (see page 145).
3. Make a flower arrangement using three kinds of materials of different sizes. Use the largest, roundest flowers near the rim of the container for a *focal area* or *center of interest* (see page 168).
4. Make a composition of *foliage and an accessory*, possibly driftwood (see page 187).
5. Go to a flower show and make quick sketches of the blue ribbon winners. Also notice the tricolor award winner. Study each for its dominant element.

A THEME ARRANGEMENT: OPPOSITES. Here are opposites in texture, color, and form. The pale green cabbage, the green banana leaves, and green container make a near-complementary color scheme with the violet-red celosia. The focal area has strong emphasis because of its round form and the contrast it offers to the darker tones. It is asymmetrical and self balanced, and the highest point is directly over the center of interest.

22

HORIZONTAL AND CIRCULAR movements are combined in the rhythm of this horizontal S arrangement of amaryllis and pine in a hollow birch log.

THE FOURSOME. As seen from above, the focal area of amaryllis flowers is located in the center; however, when seen from the side, it is at the top.

23

Chapter 4

RHYTHM

Rhythm is one of the major art principles. It is defined as *related movement*, meaning movement in line, form, pattern, or color. When rhythm in all these elements is present in an object the result is usually beauty. The design of a flower arrangement may be so rhythmic that the eye is led in a happy manner along the main lines, during which the observer is stirred, possibly excited, or merely soothed. Rhythm should lead the eye in all three dimensions, from top to bottom, from side to side, and from front to back. An arrangement without rhythm can not hold the spectator's interest long enough for him to see it thoroughly.

Growth rhythm or movement is found in all plants. Some plants point upward, some sideways, some diagonally, and some have contradictory rhythms; some grow in curves and some in straight lines. An arranger must respect the peculiarities of the plant material he or she is using. A person who wants to make an arrangement expressive of a certain flower should study the way it grows and let it follow its own rhythmic lines. When flowers are forced into lines that are not natural they do not appear happy. Subordinate materials, however, usually have to follow the rhythm of the leading plant material; the arranger should coax them to do it as gracefully as possible.

The two kinds of rhythm generally recognized in the space arts are *regular, repeated rhythm* and *free, variable rhythm*. Both are found in nature as well as in art.

Regular Repeated Rhythm. The measured beat of regular repeated rhythm is like repetition in poetry, music, or the dance. It is fundamental. Regular rhythm is more easily recognized than variable rhythm, and therefore possibly less interesting. Regular rhythm may well be featured in stylized flower arrangements used in modern settings. Regular repeated rhythm is found in radiating lines as well as in parallel lines.

Parallel rhythm is found very often in nature and might well be used more in flower arrangements. In a pine grove the straight trunks are fine examples of parallel repetition and rhythm. This is the rhythm we see in a flower bed with spike flowers rising from it. These spikes could well be cut and placed in a low container side by side as they are in the garden without having the stems converge at a single point. This effect would carry out the architectural lines of a room and enhance it decoratively (see page 30).

Free, Variable Rhythm. This kind of rhythm is related movement that is not based on regular repetition. Created examples of free variable rhythm are present in many works of art. The senses can feel a guided gliding movement in a successful painting or flower arrangement; the eye is led through all the correlated lines and masses of the composition. In flower arrangement variable rhythm is present in the line of continuity that starts at the center of interest, goes around, about, and through the plant materials and container and finally rests at the area of greatest interest again. This rhythm may be fast or slow as the designer chooses. It is usually graceful, but instead it may be dynamic and exciting (see page 101).

Nature's examples of free and variable rhythm include movement in such different things as plant materials, smoke, clouds, waves, waterfalls, birds, cats, and humans. Some plant materials have natural free, variable lines, and others may be placed in designs that have variable rhythms.

Both free rhythm and repeated rhythm may appear in the same arrangements. Even when the silhouette and linear patterns have free, variable movement, there is usually some regular repeated rhythm in the details of the flowers and leaves.

Movements. *Ascending* or *vertical* movement is featured in tall arrangements. Tall, slender materials like iris, cattail, or yucca leaves make effective vertical backgrounds. Additional rhythm results from overlapping such leaves one over the other, each one shorter than the next, or by placing each one slightly off-side in a sequence of heights. This tends to push the movement up and up. A tall container with unbroken side lines adds to ascending movement. We enjoy observing upright movement in flower arrangements because most plants naturally grow vertically (see page 236).

Horizontal movement is the most calm and restful kind of rhythm used in flower arrangements. Horizontal plant materials in a low container usually repeat the direction of the lines of the table, so that the arrangement tends to be quiet and steady. Horizontal movement is pleasing in modern rooms that feature horizontal effects in furnishings and decoration (see page 8).

Curvilinear movement is considered by many to be the most beautiful of rhythmic effects. Circular movement, as in roundish flowers, is generally desired at the center of interest in most flower arrangements; the eye goes round and round these flowers and tends to remain there. Curving stems and vines are easily arranged in beautiful line arrangements. To make complete harmonies in curves, the container and bases may also be curved, however an angular base provides transition to the angular table top or shelf (see page 130).

Diagonal or oblique movement is a very active type of movement. A strong major diagonal action requires a strong horizontal base to support it, as well as the weight of plant materials at its lower end to hold it down. An arrangement that features diagonal lines does not usually welcome any straight horizontal or vertical lines within it. It may, however, have a minor rhythm of circular or semi-circular forms at the focal area, just as some abstract paintings that feature diagonal lines have circular motifs at the center of interest for relief.

Radiating movement occurs when lines go out in several directions from one central point. The term "radiating" has pleasant connotations in flower arrangement, for it suggests alertness and activity. Radiation is considered further in the next chapter, Minor Art Principles (see page 159).

Cascading or hanging movement is natural to some plant materials, and this descending movement should be featured in their
arrangement. The rhythm of downward hanging lines is sometimes
sad and droopy in effect unless some shorter contrasting minor
rhythms of verticals, horizontals, or circles are included above the rim
of the container (see page 166).

Rhythm in Line. Twelve ways of achieving rhythm in line are
given below.

1. Use graceful curved line material and arrange it so that adjoining curves turn in the same direction.
2. Use a curved line container with curved materials.
3. Place angular materials in angular containers to repeat the
   rhythm.
4. Place straight line material in low containers in a slanting direction to get movement; for example, lean daffodils with the wind.
5. Impale all stems close together at one point on the stem holder.
6. Prune out crossing lines, especially any that are high.
7. Prune out surplus leaves and flowers for clarity of line.
8. Prune out any large leaves or flowers near the outer edges of
   an arrangement.
9. Use repetition in line, letting lesser lines follow in the general
   direction of the main line but not exactly parallel to it.
10. Keep the main movement in one direction only. Don't have
    your arrangement looking as if each side were pulling away
    from the other. Make the top of an arrangement end in one
    point only, don't let two main lines branch off like a capital Y.
11. Don't let a fast-moving leading line carry you without any break
    or brake to the edge of an arrangement and on out. Impede it
    near its base with lines going in the opposite direction.
12. Don't use loose fabrics with an arrangement unless you place
    them so that the folds will make lines that follow the rhythm,
    usually leading to the center of interest.

Rhythm in Form and Pattern. To achieve rhythm in form and
pattern requires attention to sizes and shapes, also to planes and
placement. Some suggestions are given here.

1. Use gradation in *sizes*, with large materials placed low, small

materials high, and medium materials between and overlapping the others.

2. Use gradation in *shapes*. Let the lowest flowers be round, the filler flowers or leaves oval, and the spikes pointed.

3. Overlap single leaves that are alike, making an effect like ripples, especially in stylized arrangements.

4. Overlap similar fruit or vegetables in an arrangement, turning all stem ends in the same direction.

5. Make some linear patterns inside the arrangement repeat the shape of the silhouette.

6. Let the center of interest repeat the general shape of the whole arrangement, including the voids.

7. Use some large flattish planes, like large single daisies or large leaves. Turn these planes at the sides, so as to create rhythm and third dimension.

8. Promote deep rhythm by letting some plant materials peep out from behind others.

Rhythm in Color. Although color is covered in another section (Chapter 9), a brief review of its relation to rhythm is given here. Rhythm in color may be achieved in the following ways:

1. Use analogous colors and place them in their correct sequence, as they are on the color wheel (see illustration, page 67).

2. Use gradations in value, with the darkest values lowest, and the lightest values at the top and sides, and medium values between them.

3. Use the color of the container in some flowers that are close to it.

4. Start some color areas at the outer edge and carry them down to the container, without a break.

5. Widen your color areas at the base for strength.

6. Sometimes repeat a color in two or three places in different amounts, so that the eye moves easily from one area of this color to another one like it.

7. Vary the intensity of a color, placing the least intense at the extremities and in the background areas.

8. Emphasize movement from the front to the back of the arrangement by making the back definitely lighter or darker.

PROBLEMS IN RHYTHM
(Suggestions from which to choose)

1. Draw a *curved vase* with some curved flower stems in it. Draw a *straight upright container* with straight stems in it. Draw a footed *circular bowl* with curved stems making a crescent.
2. Make an arrangement having *circular movement* only, using a round container, slightly curved line material, and round focal flowers (see page 168).
3. Make a tall arrangement having *straight ascending movement* in the background and *circular movement* at the focal area.
4. Make an arrangement with *diagonal movement* in a piece of driftwood combined with flowers, leaves, or fruit (see page 65).
5. Make an arrangement with *dominant horizontal movement* in long leaves extending sideways, and some circular movement at the central focal area (see page 8).

PARALLEL RHYTHM. Instead of radiating from one point, the gladiolus stems and leaves are set up side by side, as they grow in the garden. A row of extra stems hides the stem holder. The flowers give the effect of contrasting diagonal movement.

ANGULAR RHYTHM. The stems of the Japanese quince and the square container have similar lines and angles. The clear, well-defined silhouette has voids of various sizes and shapes that hold the interest. Camellia blossoms make a focal area that is harmonious in color and scale.

Chapter 5

THE MINOR ART PRINCIPLES

Five of the minor art principles, *repetition, transition, radiation, variation,* and *contrast,* are chosen for special study here because they apply particularly to flower arrangement. These principles overlap somewhat the major art principles. Three of them, repetition, transition, and radiation, help to produce rhythm. Variation gives interest and vitality to designs. Contrast suggests strength through opposition.

REPETITION

Although it is called a minor principle, repetition is a major factor in flower arrangement and in many other arts. As has been stated before, it is the basis of rhythmic movement. Its appeal is universal, as illustrated in the marching and dancing spectacles enjoyed by all. Repetition alone, however, is not art; the designer must control repetition and vary it. Mere repetition, like counting sheep, tends to put the observer to sleep.

In flower arrangement repetition unifies the design. Skillful arrangers repeat the leading *line*, the leading *shape*, the leading *color*, and the leading *texture* in a composition. Enough repetition of all the elements will insure *unity* even if it cannot insure beauty.

TRANSITION

Transition is easy change; gradation and sequence are progressive change. Transition is a harmonizer, a peace-maker between unlike
32

things. Easy change is pleasant, whereas an abrupt change from one extreme to another is violent; transition is like going comfortably down the stairs as compared to stepping out of a second-floor window. *Transition, gradation,* and *sequence* apply to flower arrangement in ways that have already been mentioned in this book.

A *transition in density* (solidity) is the most important application of transition in making a flower arrangement. This means that a gradual change in density usually occurs from the bottom of an arrangement to the top somewhat as follows:

1. the very dense table and container
2. the dense mass of plant materials low and at the center of interest
3. the semi-dense in-between filler materials or stem screen
4. the semi-airy spike materials
5. the airy tips of the longest spikes
6. the completely airy empty surrounding space

The dense mass of plant material at the center of interest holds the attention and should prevent the eye from passing back through the arrangement at the center of interest. A secondary material is often used as a stem screen to hide most of the openings (windows) through the lower stems. Some holes between the lower stems can be filled by placing large leaves like canna or aspidistra behind the stems that show just above the focal area.

The container, of hard permanent material, is very much unlike the plant material, which is fragile and fugitive. In order to make one unit out of these two materials it is necessary to tie them together somehow. *Transition* can be made between them by placing some of the plant material so that it extends downward over the edge of the container. Any leaves or other materials reaching over the edge must appear as though the stems are impaled on the same stem holder as the other plant materials. The eye cannot travel easily up and down the entire composition including the container, unless the straight horizontal rim of the container is partially covered. A base or mat is a transition factor between the container and the table, easing another abrupt change in form and texture.

Transition, gradation, and sequence occur in all the art elements in flower arrangement. This is explained in detail elsewhere in this book, but it bears mention here because students should learn to notice and enjoy transition in line, form, texture, and color.

RADIATION

In all decorative art, radiating motifs have been employed: the sunrays of Louis XIV and the fan windows of the Renaissance are famous examples. In flower arrangement, the most important illustration of radiation is the presently accepted theory that all lines of an arrangement should converge at one place, in one stem holder. Keeping the stems together usually gives poise and grace to a design.

Radiation is emphasized in fan-shaped arrangements, also in dome-shaped arrangements used for table centerpieces. In these, the stem holder is usually placed in the middle of a low container, and the stems radiate in many directions. Radiating arrangements of materials like small cattails can produce the effect of a big firecracker exploding.

Nature illustrates radiation in growing plants. Most flower petals and sepals radiate from center; leaves like pittosporum and loquat radiate in rosettes or whorls. The fan-palm leaf is a good example of flat radiation. The leaves of a yucca plant illustrate three-dimensional radiation.

VARIATION

Variety is always stimulating; too much sameness is monotonous and uninteresting. Naturally, we want more unity than variety, as the variation is only the seasoning in the dish. A goal in all design work is to obtain *variety within unity*. For example, the S curve design in flower arrangement has variety in its curves and in its direction, but it also has unity. Variation in color and texture as well as in line and form is essential to beauty.

In the *silhouette* of a flower arrangement variety is highly desirable: the voids and solids should make a pattern of interest. Some voids may be plain and quiet if others are patterned and exciting. In flower arrangements the background spikes are usually arranged in groups so as to produce variety in both the solids and voids. Spikes within each group are varied in length, and the entire groups are also varied in length (see page 211).

Variety in *plant materials* is essential too. The use of at least three kinds of flowers or foliage is usually desirable in an arrangement; heads, sprays, and spike materials are combined in order to get sufficient variety. An arrangement of spikes alone, sprays alone, or head flowers alone is liable to be tiresome. The eye is offended by the too frequent repetition of one form and size just as the ear would be offended by the repetition of one musical note.

Restraint in variation is also needed. Not more than five different materials should be used if unity is to be achieved in one composition. This is true of vegetable and fruit arrangements as well as flower arrangements.

There are degrees of variation too; extreme variety is needed to express certain themes and certain personalities.

CONTRAST (OPPOSITION)

Vitality is added to any composition by the inclusion of some components that contradict the main effect. For example, if a flower arrangement seems too sweet and feminine, add some strong masculine material; if an arrangement is too severe, add some softening influence (see page 86). In most flower arrangements some opposition is usually desirable in line, form, pattern, texture, and color. Well organized and controlled contrasts make strong designs.

Contrasts in line are needed in all the arts. A painting of a seascape, with all its horizontal lines, needs some verticals, as masts, trees, rocks, or people, in order to avoid monotony. The tension of lines that oppose one another is a stimulating factor in painting as well as in floral arrangement. Some plant materials have opposing movement within themselves; for example, the horizontal branches of the maple have downward-hanging winged seeds in the spring.

Contrast in form is necessary too. An arrangement consisting of sweet peas only would be entirely too insipid to be interesting. Contrasting forms like iris leaves would give it punch. Full, double flowers in a composition may need the contrast and relief afforded by large plain leaves. Avoid using several similar things together like larkspur and stock, because they make rivalry and confusion in a flower arrangement as well as in a garden (see pages 58 and 160).

Contrast in color and in *color values* is important. An arrangement in purples and lavenders that seems too retiring may need the contrast of some creamy blossoms to bring it to life. Complementary colors make the strongest possible contrasts. Dark-colored arrangements always need the contrast of light things to make them sparkle. Solid green foliage arrangements need the contrast provided by variegated foliage.

PROBLEMS IN THE MINOR PRINCIPLES
(Suggestions from which to choose)

1. Draw a picket fence. *(Mere repetition)*
   Draw the lines of a fan. *(Repetition with radiation)*
   Draw a fan shape with the lines all of different lengths and grouped to make voids of different sizes. *(Repetition, radiation, and variation)*
2. Draw a thick diagonal line rising from one end of a thick horizontal line. Draw some short opposing diagonals at the base of the strong diagonal line going in the opposite direction. *(Contrast)*
3. Draw the spokes of a long fan. Between these spokes draw other spokes that are shorter. Between them all draw even shorter spokes. At the very center make a solid black area. *(Transition in density)*
4. Make a flower arrangement that illustrates some of the five minor design principles (see page 159).
5. Make a semi-permanent arrangement with a background of groups of foliage spikes. Add temporary flowers in front (see page 211).

DOUBLE TRIANGLES. A light-colored triangle of dogwood interpenetrates a dark triangle of pittosporum. The apex of the dogwood triangle is higher than that of the pittosporum, in the manner of the plants' natural growth. Repetition is the dominant factor in this rhythm, and the many rosettes of both plant materials give a gay effect. A heavy container is needed because of the weight of the woody stems. Dogwood is not accepted in flower shows because it is listed as a conservation item, so it should only be used at home by arrangers who grow their own. In competition, a design like this one would need a more definite focal area.

TEXTURES are outstanding in this arrangement of one kind of flower. The red blossoms of *Lycoris radiata* are delicate enough to suit the exquisite carved ivory container. Repetition is featured here. The triangular form and the excellent proportions and balance are suggestive of some Japanese arrangements.

HARVEST TIME. Weathered wood provides a container for a patio table centerpiece. It has horizontal movement in contrast with the circular movement in the oats and the crinum.

PART II

The Art Elements

As a prelude to the study of the art elements, this table will show the relationship of these elements*, the art principles, and the objectives in flower and foliage arrangements.

Use these Art Elements	According to these Art Principles		To attain these Objectives
Line	Proportion	Transition	Beauty
Form	Balance	Repetition	Expressiveness
Pattern	Dominance	Radiation	Suitability
Texture	Rhythm	Variation	
Color		Contrast	

Line, form, pattern, texture, and **color** are used in flower arrangement as well as in the other visual arts. These structural elements are tangible, physical features that exist in all objects regardless of their beauty or lack of it. Each is distinct from the others, and each can be controlled by the designer to produce a desired effect. The art elements are tools that the designer must learn to handle with skill and imagination.

---

* The term "elements" should be reserved by flower arrangers to mean the *art* elements. It is confusing to call the container, stand, flowers, fruit, and background the "elements of flower arrangement." These should be known as *parts* or *components* of flower arrangement, not as elements.

Chapter 6

LINE AND FORM

LINE

The first element of art to be considered here is line. In flower arrangement beauty of line may lie in the natural, graceful lines of the plant material itself, or in the way it is arranged, or in a combination of nature and the arranger's skill. In several types of flower arrangements the line element is the dominant characteristic. Line is the basis for line arrangements, line-mass arrangements, most Japanese arrangements, and most modern arrangements.

Lines have emotional significance wherever they are used. Human beings react to line directions in the light of their own experiences. For example, when man sleeps he lies down, therefore *horizontal lines* seem restful, tranquil, and static. When man is standing upright he is alert and ready to act, therefore he considers *vertical lines* to be attentive, active, aspiring, and sometimes dignified or dramatic. When man runs he leans forward, so he feels that *diagonal lines* are full of movement and rhythm, perhaps even violence. When man is relaxed his body takes easy lines, so he considers *curvilinear lines* to be graceful and playful.

These fundamental ideas about lines are true in flower arrangement as well as in the other arts. Horizontal flower compositions are placid and restful; vertical compositions seem aspiring and alert; curvilinear arrangements appear graceful and flexible; the diagonals

40

are moving and difficult to stabilize; zigzags seem restless, dynamic and modern.

Line is closely related to form; good design depends upon how both of these elements, line and form, are used.

FORM

The term *form* here refers to the solid or three-dimensional *shape* of an entire flower arrangement. Most flower compositions that have beauty follow a carefully planned shape or form. Before choosing a form for an arrangement the designer should study her plant material, observing how it grows. Everything in nature has its own rhythm of growth: some plants have diagonal movement, some curved, and so on. The sensitive arranger tries to catch the spirit of the flower she is arranging; she does not force the material into false lines.

When an arranger is ready to decide on a basic structural design or form he or she has many from which to choose. Some typical geometric forms for flower arrangements and their subdivisions and modifications are considered here. Different forms are often *combined* to secure the shape that is wanted. The sphere, pyramid, and oblong are the basic forms, but they are seldom used without modification.

The *sphere* has many variations, such as the hemisphere (dome), circle (wheel), semi-circle, oval, semi-oval, cone, fan, crescent, lazy S (Hogarth curve), and so on.

The *pyramid* form is the basis for the half-pyramids and triangles of various kinds that are favorite shapes in American arrangements.

The *oblong* may be used vertically or horizontally. However, oblongs are usually modified and combined with other forms in making flower arrangements. Some examples are the U shapes and the Z shapes which are about equally broad at the top and the base.

Spherical or Circular Forms. A curvilinear arrangement is considered to be one of the most appealing in line and form. It usually employs plant materials that have natural graceful curves. Materials that are not curvilinear may, however, be arranged in curving patterns. Curvilinear arrangements are usually best when made in roundish containers, thereby ensuring unity of form.

The *circle* and similar shapes are considered to be serene, gentle, and satisfying. The eye follows around the design and returns to the beginning, expressing continuity and finality. The completely circular arrangement may be upright or reclining.

The *upright circular* arrangements are the one-faced type that have their backs to the wall. All lines radiate from the center of interest, which is usually located below the center of the circle. These arrangements are usually made in tall containers that allow some plant material to extend down over part of the container.

The *horizontal circular* arrangement is suitable for a dining table centerpiece; it is somewhat like a cartwheel with a raised hub. The very center may consist of a mass of round flowers which is entirely surrounded by flat radiating rays made of spike flowers like larkspur. The ends may have longer spikes than the sides as a variation, or to fit a long table. Another flat circular table centerpiece may be made of a wreath of small foliage, fruit, nuts, and possibly flowers in the manner of the bas-reliefs of the artist Della Robbia of the Italian Renaissance period. Containers are now made especially to hold such wreath-like arrangements.

The *Colonial nosegay* with its concentric circles is another example of a horizontal circular form, usually with a slight dome effect. It is sometimes called a tussy-mussy.

The *oval* is more interesting than the circle because it has some variety in its curves. The oval may be substituted for the circle in a vertical or horizontal or in any one of the other rounded arrangements described here. The egg shape is even more pleasing than the oval because of its variations.

The *hemisphere, dome,* or *half-dome* flower arrangements may be airy or compact. The compact, solid dome form is sometimes desirable for a large quantity of flowers of the same kind, which are not of superior quality. The effect is usually symmetrical and somewhat modern, for each individual flower is lost in the group design. Gradual change in color value, as from red at base to a related pink at the top, adds interest to solid domes. Small or medium-sized compact arrangements are usually preferable to large ones. Roses, daffodils, camellias, or any head flowers lend themselves to such designs.

The *airy dome or half-dome* shapes may be used for mass arrangements made in high or low containers. The use of at least three kinds of plant material together gives interest to airy mass arrangements. This is the type of free-standing arrangements so often made by florists using combinations of flower spikes, fillers, and targets. The amateur designer using this design avoids a commercial look by segregation of colors and segregation of each kind of material, and by having an uneven silhouette made by grouping the spikes so that the voids will be of different sizes. In the half-domes the back is a flat vertical plane which should be modified if possible.

A hemisphere dome arrangement with oblique curving lines, like the crossing of two croquet hoops, is an interesting complex form that is a challenge to experts. It calls especially for the third-dimensional quality that adds so much interest to a free-standing flower arrangement.

The *fan shape* has a natural feeling of growth because most plant materials radiate from a stem or trunk. The fan motif may be either gay or formal depending on its size and texture. It may be a symmetrical semi-circle, or it may be centered offside for asymmetrical balance. The fan shape shows each flower to advantage. The silhouette of a fan arrangement should usually have some large voids to prevent monotony. The semi-circular background may be a palmetto leaf, or it may be built up of groups of separate long spikes like iris, yucca, aspidistra, or ti leaves, or of spike flowers like stock, snapdragon, or lupine.

In a fan arrangement an area of interest is built up where the spokes converge at the foot of the fan. The focal area should not cover so much of the fan that the pleasing rhythm of radiation is concealed. The center of interest, too, may be somewhat circular in line; the container also is usually circular or rounded. A free-standing fan arrangement may be used as a centerpiece.

The *upright semi-circle* and *semi-oval* are popular forms in modern arrangements. The two sides are smartly contrasting in design, since the concave side of the vertical axis may be empty at the center of the semi-circle. These forms may be used for slender line arrangements or for mass effects.

The *crescent* is a graceful circular form that looks especially well in an oval bowl. Since a hairpin holder is generally needed to support the stems, the bowl should be deep enough to conceal it. A footed stand often improves the effect. The lighter end of a crescent arrangement should be higher than the slightly heavier end. In a crescent the extending material must curve upward, whether naturally or by concealed wiring, but it need not have a focal area. A crescent may be made of roses with the buds at the extremities. A crescent of slender curving juniper branches looks well with a triangle formed of five or more small apples as the area of interest. The crescent form or line suggests slow motion, for the change in direction is gradual, and it features smooth flowing lines. It has tranquility, and is pleasing for dining tables or smaller tables having some curved lines.

A *flat crescent or diadem* arrangement is easily made on a round or oval platter, tray, or large plate. It is the kind of arrangement that one must look down upon as it stands on the dining or coffee table. The floral material should of course be wider and a little higher at the center of interest, with the design tapering toward the edges and toward the points of the crescent.

Where the background of a flat arrangement is water, the sizes and shapes of the water areas are important. The flower heads should not touch the water unless they are water flowers that float naturally; other flower heads may be supported on tiny stem holders. Dahlias with philodendron, or camellias with ivy foliage, are suitable materials for flat crescents. Since single flowers from gladiolus or hollyhock spikes may be used at the focal point, a flat crescent may be economically made. A flat arrangement, while it may be pleasing in the home, is not usually suitable for a flower show.

The *long S* form is a graceful one, made of two arcs reversed. It is based on the lines of a breaking wave on the seashore, and is one of the most popular shapes in American flower arrangement. Some arrangers use this term in preference to the term "Hogarth curve," for this double curve was not the discovery of any one artist, but was used long before Hogarth's time. The long S may be horizontal or vertical or may be a combination of both, and it may vary in many other ways. The upright long S looks best in a medium-tall rounded container. The horizontal long S looks best in a low S-shaped or low oval container.

A *cone-shaped* arrangement, with the point at the top, is usually large and has either a stylized modern or a Balinese effect. The cone form may be made up entirely of inconspicuous spike flowers like white stock, around which head flowers like calla-lilies are placed in an ascending spiral, with the smallest lily at the top. Or it may be made of a solid cone of yucca leaves adorned with spirals of day-lilies. Such stylized modern arrangements should be precise in pattern and in execution.

The Balinese type is made over a wire cone base stuffed with wet sphagnum moss. It is covered with winding, ascending, parallel spirals of various small materials, such as flowers, berries, small fruits, paper decorations, and so on. The stems are stuck into the damp moss; some things are held on with florists' pins. The effect should be festive.

A cone-shaped arrangement with the point at the bottom is usually made in a cone-shaped container. Since it is often very weak at the base it may be strengthened by accessories placed near it.

Pyramids or Triangular Forms. Triangular arrangements are the most popular of all shapes. There are many kinds of triangles: the equilateral triangle has all sides equal, the isosceles has two sides equal, the scalene has no sides equal. The scalene or the isosceles may also be right-angled. Triangular arrangements are often front-faced but they can be made free-standing. Rectangular containers are desirable for triangular arrangements; however, round containers may be used for contrast (see page 51).

Symmetrical triangles are pyramids or inverted pyramids. A pyramid form is formal and dignified in effect. It is a very well balanced form, as the weight is low. The pyramid shape is the basis of the composition in many paintings by the old masters. Ultra-modern flower arrangements are often made in pyramid form, which may be tall or low depending upon the background space and the plant materials.

Asymmetrical triangular forms are of many shapes. In all of them the stem holder is placed at one side of the container. The center of interest is established directly above the stem holder. All the lines radiate from it; the tip of the tallest stem (the apex) is directly above it.

The right-angled triangle made taller than its width and resembling a sail is a popular form. The main upright line is usually a vertical but it is sometimes tipped slightly for additional movement. In the right-angled triangle the vertical may look too severe unless one or two shorter lines are placed on its left side.

A *slanting scalene triangular arrangement* (three sides different) without a horizontal or vertical line, except in the container, has a moving, exciting quality that makes it particularly suitable for a modern setting. Since it is often hard to balance, it might well be made in a low, dark container. Short opposing lines and weight at the base are needed for balance.

Japanese-type classical arrangements are triangular in two ways, the tips of the three leading lines making a triangle when seen from the front and also when seen from above. This triangular arrangement is excellent in balance, proportion and rhythm. Japanese flower arrangement is considered further in Chapter 12.

Oblong and Cubical Forms. Although there are few flower arrangements that are positively oblong or cubical, some arrangements are nearer to the oblong in shape than to the pyramid or sphere. An oblong arrangement may be horizontal, vertical, or flat in shape; its extremities usually taper and vary the geometric form considerably (see page 30).

Three-level oblongs are somewhat blocky compositions usually made of three horizontal areas, balanced by some opposing vertical areas. These arrangements constitute a definite departure from standardized forms of flower arrangements because the stems do not radiate from one spot. The stems rise from the container as they do from neighboring plants in a flower bed. To achieve this effect a low rectangular container holds several rectangular pin-point holders, some of which are farther forward than the others, allowing for overlapping planes and depth in the arrangement.

In a three-level arrangement of gladioli the uppermost line of the design usually slants downward somewhat. The middle level, which is about two-thirds the height of the top level, usually slopes down slightly toward the other side. The lowest level, which may be about one-third the height of the tallest member, may have almost no slope because it is nearest to the flat base. The effect is somewhat like the letter Z. Upright gladiolus leaves may be grouped together to make dark vertical areas rising from the base. Sections of exposed vertical stems supply the vertical movement that is needed for contrast with the horizontal levels.

Three-level arrangements of this type are distinctly architectural in effect; they repeat the horizontal and vertical lines of the room in which they stand. Unlike the usual radiating flower arrangements that are complete units within themselves, these arrangements may rather be considered as room decoration.

An L-*shaped arrangement* usually appears stable because of its strong base line. It looks best in a low rectangular container. This type is rather easy to make because the shape is clear-cut. The vertical section of the arrangement must not be the same length as the horizontal section; the proportion depends on the plant material available as well as the shape of the background space before which the arrangement will stand.

Skyscraper set-back architectural effects may be obtained in L-shapes. The background material may consist of cane, cornstalks, bamboo stalks, small birch logs, inner banana plant stalks, or similar materials.

THIRD DIMENSION

The third dimension is depth; the first and second dimensions are height and width. Depth is the difference between flat arrangements and deep arrangements, just as it is the difference between plane and solid geometry.

The form or shape of an arrangement should be considered from the front to the back as well as from side to side or from top to bottom. Arrangements that are to be seen from all sides are called *free-standing* arrangements; they usually have more depth than others.

Most flower arrangements should have depth or third dimension instead of a flat pressed look. Arrangements should have a feeling of growth, as if the stems started from one seed and freely grew out in all directions, including forward and backward, so as to get sunshine. Plants do not naturally grow flat like an espalier. Most flowers look happier if they are in arrangements that have depth.

The simplest way to obtain depth in a flower arrangement is to finish it in the back. The extra material may add several inches to the third dimension; the observer can feel the depth even if he can not actually see it (see pages 23 and 64).

Artists' Methods. Painters' methods of obtaining third dimensions may be helpful to flower arrangers. *Overlapping planes* are most effective in achieving apparent depth; they may be produced by the simple device of using leaves or flowers to hide part of another flower face, so that the flower seems to be peeping around from behind. Large stem holders allow room enough so that some plant materials may be placed well behind others, thus overlapping and giving depth.

Graded planes that gradually get darker or lighter in color from the front to the back help to carry the eye into an arrangement and produce depth. For example, a somewhat horizontal plane of hydrangea flowers might be all one color value, but it would be much more moving and three-dimensional if that one plane consisted of three values, such as pale lavender flowers at the front, medium lavender flowers in the middle, and dark lavender flowers at the back. In this same arrangement all graded planes should have similar gradation, from light at the front to dark in the back. However, in another arrangement the entire plan might be reversed with the darks in front and the lights in the back. Gradation from one hue to another in one plane in such small areas does not usually produce an appearance of depth.

A *highlight* effect can be produced in a cone or cylinder type of arrangement if it is treated as one solid form with light flowers, like a highlight, along the vertical axis, and with gradually darkening values on each side until the extreme edges are dark.

Light and shadow give a strong illusion of depth. One entire side of an arrangement may be light-colored as if a light were shining from that direction, with the other side dark and with medium values between them, producing a strong three-dimensional effect.

Advancing or receding colors may sometimes be placed so as to give a third dimension to a flower arrangement. As in a painting, the warm, advancing colors (the yellows and reds) belong in front and the cool, receding colors (the blues and their relatives) in the back, to give third dimension. Since the cool, receding colors also seem lightest in weight they can not consistently be placed lower than the warm colors. However, such refinements in color are for expert arrangers only, and for those who have many flowers from which to choose.

Receding planes are produced by turning some flowers or leaves sideways, especially at the sides of the arrangement, so as to lead the eye into the depth or third dimension.

PROBLEMS IN LINE AND FORM
(Suggestions from which to choose)

1. Draw a curved vine that changes direction and degree of curvature and tapers gradually.
2. Copy a line drawing from a Chinese or Japanese print using a pointed paintbrush and ink. Note the variety, character, and suggestion possible in a brush line.
3. Draw an abstract combination of diagonal and straight lines that suggest a flower arrangement in a low container.
4. Draw an equilateral, an isosceles, and a scalene triangular outline for flower arrangements and suitable containers for each one.
5. Make a horizontal foliage arrangement to place on a TV cabinet over which a painting is hung.
6. Make a tall, slim, vertical, semi-circular, C-shaped arrangement in a tall container (see page 84).
7. Make a triangular flower arrangement (see page 57).

SPIRAL ASCENDING MOVEMENT. Purple Dawn camellias placed around the core of a banana tree stalk make a dramatic stylized arrangement. The flowers are pinned to the stalk with common pins, the smallest at the top. An occasional spray of mist keeps them fresh. Double hibiscus or day-lilies might also be used. Reminiscent of Balinese decorations, this vertical arrangement stresses circular lines in plant materials, container, and base.

TRIPLE TRIANGLES of snapdragons, callas, and dark iris.

THE THIRD DIMENSION. The upper chrysanthemums reveal depth.

Chapter 7

PATTERN

The term *pattern* as used in flower arrangement refers to the two-dimensional shapes of things; it means somewhat the same as decorative design, and is closely related to the Japanese art term *notan* (dark and light pattern). In a flower arrangement, pattern may refer to the *silhouette* or outer shape of the entire arrangement, to the *linear and mass patterns* within the body of the composition, or to the separate *shapes of the plant materials* that are used.

The Silhouette. The word silhouette comes from the name of a very stingy eighteenth-century minister of finance in France. Originally silhouette referred to the most economical portrait possible, an outline filled in with solid black. Today this term may refer to a solid shadow picture of any object or to the outer edges of any area.

The silhouette of a flower arrangement means the pattern made by its outside outline as seen against a background. The flowers and leaves at the outside edges of the arrangement form the *solid areas* of the pattern, and the background spaces or indentations between the plant materials form the *voids*. In analyzing the pattern of the silhouette of a flower arrangement a designer must consider the shapes of both the solids and the voids.

The *voids* are considered important in all the arts. Painters treat the voids in their pictures as negative volume and organize them thoughtfully. Architects consider the shapes of the space areas and the openings in buildings as carefully as they do the solid areas.

52

Flower arrangers, too, consider the voids or openings in their compositions as design problems. Arrangers create voids in the silhouette by leaving empty spaces between the plant materials, by pruning, and by cutting stems in different lengths.

Regular, repeated spacing of plant material is precise and machine-like and may look well in modern rooms. Sansevieria, yucca, and aspidistra leaves lend themselves to this effect. In most arrangements, however, *irregular voids* are preferable, for variety is pleasing even in the shape and size of empty spaces. *Small, medium, and large voids* are found in most arrangements. The largest voids are usually in the upper part of an arrangement; however, a void should never occur at the center of the top. Voids that are too large in a mass arrangement tend to break the design apart. Open spaces should not usually be allowed near the lower, central core of an arrangement, where density is desirable.

Plain-edged voids and *broken-edged voids* in the same arrangement help to make it interesting. Yucca or iris leaves may well be used near leafy branches to give variety.

Flower arrangements without sufficient voids are apt to look stuffy. Airy arrangements show the natural lines of the plant materials to better advantage.

Linear and Mass Patterns. The main body of a studied flower arrangement, inside the silhouette, should usually be composed of definite patterns made by the careful placement of plant materials. Usually each material is segregated and placed where it is most effective. Studied gradations in size, color, and texture are employed. When creating the patterns in the body of an arrangement the designer often tries to follow some of the lines of the silhouette or general shape of the entire composition. For example, in a *circular arrangement* made in a round container most of the linear and mass patterns would be curvilinear. In such a rounded design it would be unthinkable to use a straight horizontal branch or a straight row of flowers or even a long straight diagonal, although some short diagonals might look well at the center of interest. A curve, within a curve, within a curve, within a curve, is a graceful idea.

In a *triangular arrangement* the inside patterns may also be slightly triangular in part, and the center of interest may suggest another triangle, thus insuring unity. Diagonal drifts often make pleasing linear patterns in triangular arrangements; they can be controlled to suggest movement in the direction desired.

Plant Materials.   To get interesting patterns throughout a flower arrangement, a designer often employs a variety of sizes and shapes in plant materials. Many arrangements include all three of the main shapes, *spikes*, *sprays*, and *head flowers*. Most flowers and foliage seem to fall into one of these general classes.

Spikes are long, slender, tapering materials, which may be curved or straight. They give height, width, airiness, and background to an arrangement. Spike flowers include gladiolus, larkspur, wallflower, lupine, stock, watsonia, and delphinium; spike leaves include iris, yucca, sansevieria, and ti. Spikes may also consist of buds, berries, seed pods, or any other natural, extending material. The spikes are often placed on the stem holder first; they may form the background skeleton and the outline that determines the size and shape of the design.

Spray materials include leaves like pittosporum, and flowers like ageratum that have lateral sprays. Such materials are used for filler areas in mass arrangements; they help to give volume and third dimension. They also serve as the medium size in gradations between large and small flowers or leaves. The term "filler" is probably less desirable than the term "secondary materials." Seed pods, small fruit, or berries may also serve in this way. Other spray flowers are small chrysanthemums, asters, and goldenrod. Some leaves that may be used as fillers are nandina, camellia, box, cedar, pine, peony, and yew. Fillers are seldom used in modern arrangements, line arrangements, or in Japanese arrangements, because fillers are likely to interfere with the clarity of line required in the design of these arrangements.

Head or *terminal flowers* are those that usually grow at the end of stems, such as roses, zinnias, calendulas, asters, carnations, lilies, and iris. The fairly large round head flowers are the best materials to use at the center of interest in a flower arrangement. They attract and hold the observer's attention. Such flowers are also useful as weight material; they are often placed low to help stability. It is easy to control the position of a single flower on the end of a stem.

Leaves that grow in natural rosettes, such as hen-and-chickens, constitute the best focal area material in a foliage arrangement. Variegated pittosporum leaves, also geranium, hydrangea, fancy caladium, croton, coleus, loquat, and magnolia, are likewise useful. Croton leaves may be overlapped and pinned around the top end of a carrot to make a good focal rosette resembling a huge flower.

Plain planes are necessary in a flower arrangement as a contrast to the busy flowered areas. Many flower arrangements appear restless because, except for the container, they have no plain surfaces on which to rest the eyes. It is often desirable to use large flattish leaves below the flowers at the center of interest to give relief, to help cover the rim, and to provide weight. Especially suitable leaves are the begonia, geranium, galax, caladium, calla-lily, sycamore, tung, magnolia, and loquat.

Table Settings. Pattern should always be considered when making or judging a table setting; it is the most important art factor present. Beauty in the pattern of table settings depends upon several different points.

(1) The *proportion of patterned surfaces* to plain surfaces in the entire assemblage of a table setting must be pleasing. A reasonable relationship is to have three-fourths of the surfaces plain and one-fourth patterned. In very modern settings it is desirable to have the cloth and all the other appointments plain, with the pattern provided by flowers and food.

(2) All the patterns that appear on the linens, silver, china and glassware should *agree in scale*. It would be unpleasant to see large patterns in the tablecloth and tiny patterns on other appointments.

(3) All the patterns that are used on the fabrics, flatware, china and glassware should *agree in style*. For example, Wedgwood china may be used with any of the Neoclassical silverware patterns, like Adam, Sheraton, Hepplewhite, Louis XVI or Pompeiian, but it should not be used with Louis XIV or any other baroque or rococo patterns.

(4) The decorative *patterns* should have beauty in themselves.

The most discerning buyers know the names of the foremost designers and try to procure their work. Restraint is usually a mark of quality in dishes as well as in dresses.

(5) The *forms* of dishes, glasses, and hollow silver pieces should be related somewhat and should have beauty within themselves, irrespective of any decoration. Angles and extreme shapes are usually inconsistent with the art of the potter or the glass-blower, whose products are naturally roundish.

(6) The *floral centerpiece* or other floral decoration becomes the focal area of the entire pattern of the table. The center decoration on a table should usually be contained within the central one-third of the length and one-third of the width of the table. Smaller multiple arrangements sometimes make a better pattern than one centerpiece.

(7) *All the appointments* on the table should constitute a distinctive pattern. They must be placed with regard for balance, emphasis, and rhythm. Fairly even distribution of weight is desirable. Emphasis should be on the floral decoration. Rhythmic lines should carry the eye to the centerpiece, then around among the articles, and finally back to the largest floral decoration.

PROBLEMS IN PATTERN
(Suggestions from which to choose)

1. Draw some leaves that have definite and interesting pattern, as fern, aralia, sassafras, acanthus, Hercules club, or barberry.
2. Study paintings of jungle foliage by Emile Rousseau, a French artist.
3. Make an arrangement using strongly patterned foliage as background (see page 168).
4. Make an arrangement in which the flower heads are placed in precise patterns (see page 86).
5. Draw a plan for a table setting for any meal, showing the location of the various appointments.
6. Make a low, symmetrical flower arrangement to use as a dining-table centerpiece. Locate pictures showing the table equipment that would look well with your arrangement. Show your color scheme with colored papers, paints, or crayons.

NATURE'S PATTERNS. The mood is gay; the many radiating lines are lively. Pink, white, and green are vigorous complements that compel attention. The date palm leaves have been trimmed to the right proportions, and the lightest and largest amaryllis flower has been placed at the bottom, where the stem lines meet. The English container is of beautiful greenish metal.

57

TEXTURES IN FRUIT AND FOLIAGE. This smooth gourd container harmonizes with the fresh fruit and contrasts with the crinkled paper-plant leaves. The wooden base has the sturdy quality that suits all these materials. This composition is a modified triangle open at the right side. The focal area is located near the point of the triangle where the largest fruit is concentrated. The leaves make patterns that repeat the dark shapes of the heartwood in the base, which is a slice across the trunk of a cypress tree. Natural indentations in a base are interesting but artificial indentations that do not even follow the grain of the wood are meaningless.

58

Chapter 8

TEXTURE

Texture is another important element of art. Texture in plant materials is determined by their tactile *surface quality* and by their *tissue structure*. Even the pliability or rigidity and the thickness or thinness of plant materials have textural significance.

Appreciation of texture in general has increased recently due to its promotion by modern painters, landscape architects, and interior decorators. Flower arrangers should seriously study the use of texture in achieving beauty. Many women are naturally sensitive to textures, yet there are some who would put a dry arrangement on a lace tablecloth although they would be shocked at the use of calfskin oxfords with a lace dress.

Plant materials have extreme variations in textures. Some flowers of interesting texture are gardenias, carnations, ranunculas, geraniums, tritomas, foxgloves, coxcombs, and sunflowers. Artichokes, pineapples, pine cones, and dock have unusual textures. Expert flower arrangers know that an insipid flower arrangement may be saved by the addition of a strongly textured material. In flower shows texture is especially important, for it often produces the distinction that wins the blue ribbons. Unpleasant textures such as thistles or century plants that might injure the arranger or the unwary observer are inexcusable in a flower show and are seldom used in a home.

Appreciation of the wealth of texture variations in natural materials is one of the important benefits to be derived from the study of flower arrangement. Collecting natural materials with unusual textures like seed pods, rocks, shells, and old wood is a fine family hobby.

Flower arrangers who wish to use texture most intelligently must give it thought in order to understand its subtleties. Arrangers should be interested in learning the precise words to use in describing a specific texture. The following is a list of words that apply to textures.

airy	dewy	hard	ridged	solid
bearded	downy	harsh	rigid	spongy
bristly	dull	lacy	rough	sticky
burnished	feathery	leathery	rubbery	stiff
coarse	fine	light	sandy	thorny
corky	firm	metallic	satiny	tough
crackled	flexible	mossy	scaly	twisted
crepy	frilly	nettled	scratchy	unpolished
crinkly	furry	pebbly	shiny	velvety
crisp	fuzzy	polished	silky	warty
curly	glossy	powdery	sleek	waxy
delicate	grooved	prickly	smooth	woody
dense	hairy	ribbed	soft	woolly

As the term is used in flower arrangement, texture has little to do with the size of plant materials. Small size does not necessarily indicate fine texture. For example, boxwood is small but not fine textured, whereas maidenhair fern is small and also fine textured.

Some plants and other materials have in themselves two contrasting textural qualities, both of which must be considered in arranging them. For example, the magnolia leaf is shiny and smooth but its tissue structure makes it heavy and hard. Loquat leaves are rougher but are not as tough as magnolia, therefore they may be used with materials somewhat finer than magnolia. White coral has rough texture but it expresses fragility, and so it is pleasing with flowers that are refined in texture, as well as with some that are not.

Agreement in texture between container and the plant materials used in it is a fairly obvious requirement. For example, fine and medium glass containers are suitable for delicate flowers like sweet peas, gypsophila, columbines, cosmos, lobelia, or poppies. Very heavy glass is consistent with coarser materials. Heavy pottery is agreeable with sturdy or coarse flowers like calendulas, ageratum, and some zinnias. Fine glazed pottery suits most flowers, even those that are velvety and luxurious. Heavy pottery, wood, or metal containers are advisable for heavy, coarse, or dry materials. In fact, a metal container usually calls for some strength in flowers, like woody stems or large materials. Silver is luxurious and is therefore used with rich velvety surfaces, such as dahlias and roses.

Agreement in texture among the plant materials must also be considered fully. For example, canna leaves are better in texture and size with gladioli than the gladiolus leaves are. Calendulas are heavy-looking and marguerites are airy, so they do not combine well. Although most lilies are considered to be velvety and fine, the tiger lily is an exception and combines well with sturdier materials. In mass arrangements all the flowers usually agree in texture; in the line or line-mass arrangements more variety in texture is possible. Most flowers should be studied before they are classified texturally. See page 93 for some classifications.

Agreement in textures between fabrics and other materials used in a flower arrangement is usually desirable: for example, velvet is not suitable for heavy pottery; nylon is not agreeable with driftwood; monk's cloth is not friendly with glass. A gingham cloth is not suitable for velvety roses or dahlias; grass table mats should not be used with poppies in glass vases; and lace cloths certainly do not agree with brittle dry materials and ordinary metal containers. Throughout any *table setting* agreement in texture is usually necessary if harmony is to be procured among the many miscellaneous appointments that are assembled.

Agreement in texture among all materials in an arrangement is often necessary if the arranger is trying to *express one single idea.* There are exceptions to this also: for example, although a "Beachcomber's Arrangement" might well have driftwood and shells together, texturally these materials are quite different. The shiny shells have hard, clean-cut lines, and the driftwood has soft, irregular edges, and a worn look.

Contrast in texture, on the other hand, may be featured in certain flower arrangements, as modern arrangements, monochromatic ar-

rangeme
desirabl
emphasi
a smoot
rials cor
smooth
culine.
both ma
to creat
other te
trasts ai
tulips;
A class
any na
domina
plies te:
Whe
a *transi*
are to
needed,
the arr
such as
loquat
ture ai
camelli
and da
ner an
are fin
to proc

1. Mal
   page
2. Mal
   husl

Chapter 9

COLOR

One of the most important elements of art is *color*. The enjoyment of color is largely an emotional process felt by even the most primitive peoples. On the other hand, the appreciation of line and form is a more intellectual process that is not so commonly experienced. Nearly everyone responds to color to a certain extent. The person who is trained in the theory and the use of color, however, obtains more pleasure from it than the untrained.

The Source of Color. *Light* is the source of all color; in darkness there is no color. All objects reflect light which enters the eyes, stimulates the optic nerve, and causes in the brain the sensation we call color. Light rays or waves which vary in length and rate of vibration produce different sensations and consequently different colors. A beam of light which contains all the fundamental colors can be broken up by means of a spectroscope, a glass prism, or a diamond, so that all the spectrum colors are revealed, much as in the rainbow. At one edge of the spectrum is violet, which has the shortest visible waves; at the other edge is red, which has the longest visible waves. Between the violet and the red are blue, green, yellow, and orange, produced by the varying intermediate waves. In the natural spectrum the hues blend imperceptibly; there are no separate bands of color. In our study of color, however, we separate the hues and arrange them in a wheel.

Objects reflect part of a light beam and absorb other parts: for example, a green object is reflecting green, and absorbing all the other colors that make up white light; a white object is reflecting all the colors that make up light; a black object is absorbing all the colors and reflecting none. This fact helps to explain why white garments or houses are the most comfortable for hot, sunny climates.

THEORIES OF COLOR

The theories of color used in chemistry, physics, psychology, and art are presented here very briefly. Each one of these fields employs a different color theory because each is concerned with different aspects of the study of color.

The Pigment Theory of Color. The accompanying figure illustrates the principles of the pigment theory of color. This theory is the most practical basis for mixing paints and for learning

PIGMENT THEORY WHEEL WITH 18 HUES

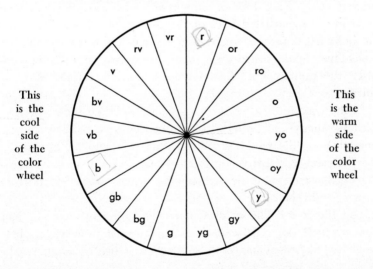

This is the cool side of the color wheel

This is the warm side of the color wheel

color harmony in flower arrangement. In the pigment theory the *primary colors* are *red, yellow, and blue*; these primary colors cannot themselves result from the mixing of any other colors. However, the primary colors, in pigments, can be mixed to make the *secondary colors: orange, green, and violet.* Orange is obtained by mixing red and yellow, green by mixing yellow and blue, and violet by mixing red and blue. These six colors—red, orange, yellow, green, blue, and violet—are known as the standard colors. *Tertiary or intermediate colors* are obtained by mixing a primary color with its nearest secondary color on the color wheel.

The color wheels that illustrate the pigment theory usually consist of six, twelve, or eighteen hues. The eighteen-hue wheel is used by many flower arrangement teachers; however the twelve-hue wheel is simpler and equally useful unless one wishes to differentiate between such close hues as violet-red and red-violet.

The *twelve-hue wheel* shows the six standard colors and six tertiary colors. The tertiary colors are named for the hues on both sides of them, for example the color between green and yellow is called green-yellow. The first color named in a hyphenated hue is considered to be only a modifier of the second color, therefore the primary color, being the more important, is here used as the second color in the hyphenated hues of the twelve-hue wheel. These hues are violet-red, orange-red, orange-yellow, green-yellow, green-blue, and violet-blue. Some instructors prefer to reverse these names and place the primary hues first; either position is considered to be correct.

In the *eighteen-hue wheel* two separate hues are shown between each secondary and primary color. Between green and yellow the hue adjoining the yellow is called green-yellow and the hue adjoining the green is called yellow-green. Green-yellow is more yellowish than yellow-green. In the eighteen-hue wheel twelve of the color names are hyphenated.

The Physicist's Theory of Color. The primary colors in light (not pigment) are red (scarlet), green (emerald), and violet (blue-violet). The secondary colors are yellow (slightly orange), blue (cyan), and red-violet (magenta). The secondary colors are produced by combining colored light, using two of the primary colors. The complementary or opposite colors if thrown together on a screen will neutralize each other and produce white light. A similar result will be obtained by projecting the three primaries on a screen together.

The Psychologist's Theory of Color. This theory is based on the visual perception of color. Red, green, yellow, and blue are the four fundamental or primary colors used in this theory. Orange, yellow-green, blue-green, and violet are the four secondary colors. Colors that are opposite one another on the color wheel are called complementary. A top on which is painted a pair of these complements will appear while twirling to be a pure gray. According to this theory, a very simple method of determining which color is complementary to another is to look for 30 seconds at a colored disk against a white background. At the end of that time, when the disk is removed, a round spot of the color that is complementary to the one removed will immediately appear in its place, as an after-image. Psychologists have developed color therapy fairly extensively.

The Munsell Color System. This system of *color notation* makes it possible to describe precisely the hue, value, and chroma of any color. In the Munsell system there are five major (primary) hues: yellow, green, blue, purple, and red, and five minor (secondary) hues. The complementary colors are yellow and purple-blue, green and red-purple, blue and yellow-red, purple and green-yellow, red and blue-green. As an example of notation by this system, standard red is R 4/10. This is the symbol for a 4 value and a 10 chroma (intensity) of red.

QUALITIES OF COLOR

Color has three qualities or dimensions that can be measured with considerable exactness.

Hue. The words *hue* and *color* are practically synonymous, the hue and the name of a color are the same. The hues or colors in the 18-hue wheel are: red, orange-red, red-orange, orange, yellow-orange, orange-yellow, yellow, green-yellow, yellow-green, green, blue-green, green-blue, blue, violet-blue, blue-violet, violet, red-violet, and violet-red. A hue retains its name even though it is lighter, darker, or grayer than the normal or spectrum hue. Two exceptions to this are pink which is light red and lavender which is light violet.

Value. Value refers to the *lightness or darkness* of colors. The lightest possible value is white, the darkest value is black; there are many values between white and black. The diagram below shows ten different grays between black and white. Similar neutral value scales, however, may have fewer or more values of gray. On the scale below each of the normal spectrum colors, as found in the rainbow, is placed adjoining its corresponding value of gray. Normal yellow is the lightest value in the spectrum colors and normal violet is the darkest. When comparing values you should almost close your eyes and squint, for this helps to shut out color and emphasizes value.

	Neutral value scale	*Spectrum hues*	
	1 white		
Light values	2		
	3_____	standard	yellow
	4_____	"	orange
	5		
Medium values	6		
	7_____	"	green
	8_____	"	red
	9_____	"	blue
Dark values	10_____	"	violet
	11		
	12 black		

In mixing paints white is added to any hue to make *tints* or *light values*, for tints are lighter than the spectrum hues. Black is added to any hue to make *shades* or *dark values*, for shades are darker than the spectrum hues. Instead of black other hues may be used to darken the light hues. Such additions, however, would alter the hue and chroma of a color as well as the value. Flower arrangers should learn to use the terms light or dark values rather than tints or shades, which are so often used incorrectly.

Many artists like to use hues at about their normal value, as in the spectrum, in their paintings, for they think that colors are most effective at normal value even when they are grayed. For example, since standard violet is dark, a pale violet tint has some connotations of artificiality, according to some painters.

When *expressing certain ideas* in flower arrangements the most effective value should be employed. Light colors are generally lyrical and uplifting; dark colors are rich and dramatic. Light values seem to increase the size of an area. Close values are restful; decided differences in value are lively. Value contrasts are necessary for effective black and white photographs of flower arrangements.

Intensity (Chroma).   Intensity refers to the *brightness or dullness* of colors, regardless of their values. The true spectrum colors have full chroma or intensity, as true red, true orange, or true blue. To reduce the intensity (or purity) of a color, add to it either gray or some of its complementary color. It is practically impossible to indicate any change in intensity in the darker values of a color.

Reduced colors are, of course, more subtle than pure colors. The popular term for colors that have been reduced in intensity is soft colors. In flower arrangement, the intense colors suggest exotic effects, while the subdued colors, especially the lighter values, suggest traditional effects.

Tone is used by some colorists to describe a color that has been subdued by the addition of gray. The word tone is a good one, for it carries the idea of being toned down. Toned colors are usually pleasing. A tint tone is a light color that is grayed. A shade tone is a dark color that is grayed. In mixing paints it is often desirable to tone down a color by adding to it its own complement, which subdues it without making it chalky; however it does change the hue.

Warmth or Coolness.   We probably feel that certain colors are warm or cool because we associate them with objects that are warm or cool. Red and yellow seem warm to us because they are the colors of fire and sunshine. Blue and green seem cool because they are the colors of skies, water, ice, and foliage.

The color wheel can be divided almost into halves with the cool colors on one side, the warm ones on the other side, and a borderline color between them. If red is placed at the top of the wheel, all the hues on the yellow side from red to green are warm. The hues on the other side from violet-red through blue to green are cool. Since green is made by mixing blue with yellow, green may be either warm or cool; when yellow dominates the result is a warm yellow-green; when more blue is used the result is a cool blue-green.

In a flower arrangement or a table setting, either the cool or the warm colors should dominate; equal quantities of each are not desirable. All the warm colors are harmonious with one another because they belong to the yellow-red family; the cool colors are harmonious with one another because they are related to the blue family. The cool colors are apparently lighter in weight than the warm colors, therefore one should consider placing the blues and violets at the top of an arrangement with the heavy yellows and reds at the bottom and the middle-weight greens between. Blue is not a desirable color for a container, unless the flowers are mostly blue and white.

Advancing and Receding Colors. The warm hues seem to advance toward the observer, the cool hues to recede. The most advancing color is yellow, then orange, red, green, violet, and blue in order. Intense colors advance more than those that are grayed.

These qualities of advancement or recession must be considered in flower arrangement. For example, it is unwise to place orange flowers in a blue bowl, because the bowl and flowers will not seem to remain in the same vertical plane, the flowers will advance and the bowl retreat; therefore, unity between the two is difficult. The same would be true of yellow flowers in a violet container.

Acid and Earth Colors. An arbitrary division separates the acid colors from the earth colors. The acid colors, made from chemical (analine) products, include carmine, magenta, some violets, cyan blue, and blue green. The earth colors, which are mostly warm, are made from earth or vegetable products. They include the warm reds, yellow, ochre, sienna, umber, and sap green. The earth and the acid colors are not harmonious and should not usually be combined. For example, pure magenta and pure yellow are not friendly.

EXPRESSIVENESS IN COLORS

Colors express certain ideas to which we respond emotionally. The early Christian church used colors to convey messages to people who could not read. White was for innocence, black for evil or death, gray for penitence, red for love, bravery, or martyrdom, and blue for sincerity and hope. The theatre has carried on the same color symbolism up to the present time. However, colors have many additional connotations today.

Yellow, the color of the sunlight and some artificial light, is gay, exultant, cheerful, optimistic, youthful, and sympathetic. It reflects more light than other colors. It is especially desirable in flower arrangements for dark locations such as halls.

Orange, the most vivid and vibrant of all hues, expresses action. It is energetic, courageous, spirited, hopeful, and cordial. Only small areas of brilliant orange should ordinarily be used, but neutralized forms of orange, like salmon, rust, and copper colors, may be used in large areas. In flower arrangements the modified orange colors, including brown, are expressive of autumn.

Brown, which may be a dark yellow, dark orange, or dark red, depending on its content, is restful, gentle, tranquil, humble, mellow, and down-to-earth. In flower composition, brown appears most often in dry arrangements. It is a very satisfactory color for containers.

Red, a favorite and powerful hue, is the color of fire and blood. It is warm, strong, exciting, passionate, vigorous, dangerous, bold, forceful, hospitable, exhilarating, and splendid. Red has opposite meanings: to a lover or a poet it suggests love; to a motorist it means danger; to primitive man it meant the fire at the entrance to his cave, a beacon of safety. Pink, which is diluted red, is a favorite color with many women.

In flower arrangement the standard red should usually be used with the warm colors, not with the cool, except in patriotic red, white, and blue schemes. Red carries well over distances, so it is usually desirable in arrangements in large rooms. It looks well by artificial light.

Magenta (violet-red) has a feeling of richness, solidity, and luxury. It is associated with the Victorian Age. Raspberry and maroon are forms of magenta. Magenta is considered a cool red, and fits into cool harmonies because it is friendly to all the blues. On the other hand, magenta is unhappy in warm schemes and pure yellow is particularly unpleasant with it.

Purple, a little warmer than violet, is gentle, vague, mysterious, dignified, reflective, philosophic, and sad. Royal purple also suggests splendor.

Violet has sentimentality, refinement, and modesty, and suggests age. It is a peace maker in a color scheme.

Blue, the color of skies and deep water, is cool, distant, dignified, calm, serene, formal, and restrained. Blue expresses loyalty and truth, as "true blue."

Green, the most plentiful color in nature, is the color of coolness, rest, and freshness. It is refreshing, calm, and healing. Arrangements expressing coolness in flower shows are often made in green or green and white.

Black, a neutral which is not often found in plant materials, is mysterious, sophisticated, dramatic, interesting, masculine, and cold.

White, the absence of color, is cool, clean, pure, delicate, feminine, serene, and uplifting.

Gray, the most gentle of the neutrals, seems quiet, serene, restrained, prim, mild, soft, neutral, cooperative, adaptable, and dignified. Gardeners should grow plants with gray foliage to blend colors in the garden and to use in cool-colored flower arrangements.

Neutral colors include black, white, and gray. Colorists say that none of these are really colors, that they are merely the absence of color; in general usage, however, they are known as colors.

COLOR HARMONY

It would be best if every person could develop his or her own sense of color gradually through experience, but life is too busy and too brief for such experimentation. A sense of color harmony is natural to some people, but most of us must study this subject to get the best results.

There are unlimited numbers of color schemes, although only a few have been standardized and are commonly used by students. Trained artists can harmonize any and all colors through the necessary adjustments.

Nature's color schemes are plentiful too. They are found in flowers, fruits, vegetables, rocks, fishes, and in many other sources. However, it must not be assumed that all nature's color schemes are suitable to copy in flower arrangements.

Beginners' color harmony study may start with a simple plan that is very useful until individual color sense develops. This guidance plan is to use together only the cool colors or the warm colors, without mixing them.

Standard Color Schemes. Two *pigment color theory* wheels containing twelve hues or eighteen hues are used in the explanation of the following color schemes. Only the six standard color schemes that are used most often are presented here. When these schemes are called for in schedules of flower shows certain restrictions or interpretations are generally understood. Some of them are listed here. In all the standard schemes if *leaves* are used in arrangements their colors cannot be ignored, and they must fit correctly into the color scheme that is required in the class. *Green stems* are acceptable in any scheme, but an area of green stems used as a definite integral part of the pattern is not allowed unless the required color scheme includes green. *Green tip ends* of snapdragons and similar flowers should be permissible in any scheme. Flowers with very noticeable *yellow centers* should not be used in standard color schemes in flower shows unless the scheme includes yellow. Small *incidental bits* of unwanted color are acceptable in any of the standard color schemes.

The *neutrals white, gray, and black* are supposed to be colorless and are therefore technically acceptable in any standard color scheme. The sensitive colorist, however, usually finds that gray or black disturbs the rhythm in an analogous scheme, that white is unpleasant in a complementary scheme, and that black is distracting as a container unless something black is used in the composition.

Related harmonies and *unrelated harmonies* are terms used to describe the standard color schemes. The related harmonies are the monochromatic and analogous, the unrelated harmonies are the direct complementary, split-complementary, and triadic schemes. We prefer the term schemes to the term harmonies, because unfortunately the results do not always turn out to be harmonies.

In *flower shows* there is a tendency to omit the standard color scheme classes from the schedules and to substitute less limiting classes. For example, instead of having the class description call for a monochromatic in red, it is now considered better to call for an arrangement with emphasis on red. This will give the judges more freedom to look for beauty, not for minor violations of schedule requirements.

A Monochromatic Color Scheme. Only one color may be used in this scheme, but any of the tints or shades of this color may be included. The neutral colors may be added, however. Strong dark and light contrasts are desirable in monochromatics. Interest is gained by emphasis on the other elements, as varied textures and bold forms, since color is so restrained.

The most common use of the monochromatic color scheme is for dry brown and tan arrangements and for fresh green foliage arrangements. A tall green monochromatic with special form and textural interest can be made in a green pottery container by using straight pine branches for the tallest element, and some broader green leaves such as oak or cottonwood for weight, with a center of interest consisting of green fruit on its stems or seed pods like green cockleburs.

Yellow combinations are particularly desirable for monochromatics in the autumn when yellow leaves are plentiful. They look well in brass or brown (considered yellow) pottery containers. Purple plum foliage, purple cabbage, and purple fruit are all interesting possibilities for monochromatic use, possibly with gray driftwood in a gray container. A pleasing red-violet monochromatic arrangement consists of red-violet gladioli, red-violet water-lilies, and red-violet leaves in a red-violet glass container. In a copper container a handsome monochromatic arrangement can be made of two different values of orange gladioli and a large dark orange dahlia.

Monochromatic arrangements are especially desirable in rooms that have sufficient or too much variety in color and pattern. Then your eye leaves the variations and rests on the one-color effect. If you want to bring out some particular color in a picture, put a monochromatic arrangement of that color beneath it. Monochromatics are also desirable for use in rooms that are too sunny. All-green arrangements or other monochromes are useful as additional arrangements in a room where you already have a big colorful flower arrangement.

An Analogous Color Scheme. *Adjoining colors* on the color wheel are combined in this scheme. Not more than *one primary color* or more than *one third of the color wheel* may be used in an analogous scheme. Some teachers claim that the analogous sequence must have a primary color for one end, but the meaning of the word doesn't indicate such a limitation. In an analogous scheme it is considered best to include four or five hues from the twelve-hue wheel; more hues may be used from the eighteen-hue wheel. Neighboring colors have the effect of taming one another.

As in all other color schemes, it is necessary to have *one color dominate* in order to unify the total effect of a flower arrangement. The arranger should experiment with several tints and shades of this dominant hue, adding at least three neighboring hues to form an analogous harmony. Three hues are better than two, just as three notes in a chord are usually better than two.

In an analogous arrangement, place the colors in their *correct sequence,* as they are on the color circle, so as not to spoil the rhythm. For example, do not put orange between orange-yellow and yellow, but let orange-yellow be in the middle. It is permissible to omit a color in a sequence when making an analogous arrangement, because of the difficulty of procuring flowers that are right in color and size.

Two favorite analogous combinations from the twelve-hue wheel are: (1) green-yellow, yellow, orange-yellow, orange; (2) violet-red, violet, violet-blue, blue. Not all adjoining colors make good analogous schemes. For example, green-blue and violet-red each look better with their adjoining cooler colors. Like all color schemes, an analogous scheme usually should be predominantly cool or warm, this is very easy to achieve when using neighboring colors.

An analogous scheme in flower arrangements is especially good for the home, as it is quiet and pleasant for close-up views. Many colorists consider this the most desirable of all color combinations.

An entertaining idea about analogous color schemes is that each season of the year seems to feature colors that make an analogous scheme with the colors of the next season. Spring is green and yellow-green; summer is yellow and yellow-orange; autumn is orange, red, and brown; winter is brown, violet, bluish gray and blue; these sequences have taken us around the entire color wheel, as well as around the seasons.

A Direct Complementary Color Scheme. The two colors that are directly opposite one another on the color wheel are complementary. Any pair of these hues and/or their tints or shades constitute a complementary scheme. In the flower arrangements in most flower shows it is best to interpret the term complementary broadly, letting any red be considered complementary to any green, for the average garden does not have a great range of colors from which to choose. It is not enough to have one of the complementary colors showing in the container only; that color should be repeated somewhere in the plant materials to produce a unified effect (see page 168).

Complementary colors enhance one another's brilliance. For example, close proximity of orange makes blue seem bluer than otherwise. Complementary colors complete one another; one fills the other out. They have the strongest possible contrast; they demand our attention. They express boldness and possibly antagonism.

Red and green is a favorite complementary scheme at Christmas time. However, the tertiary colors like orange-red and green-blue make more subtle complementary schemes. Some arrangers use yellow and violet together, but most artists today prefer the more subtle green-yellow and violet-red. Some of nature's striking complementary combinations are purple iris with yellow centers, orange birds-of-paradise with central dashes of blue, and poinsettias of red and green.

One of a pair of complementary colors should greatly dominate in quantity; the one of which there is a smaller quantity usually being the more intense. The color that dominates in quantity should not be alike all through the arrangement; light, medium, and dark values are desirable in the dominant hue, and usually there is more of the light value than the dark.

A complementary scheme carries well, and is often used for distant effects in large rooms, such as churches or halls, as well as in flower shows.

Complementary schemes that are based on the twelve-hue wheel or the eighteen-hue wheel are about the same for all practical purposes in flower arrangement.

Some complements in the twelve-hue wheel	*Some complements in the eighteen-hue wheel*
yellow and violet	yellow and violet
green-yellow and violet-red	green-yellow and red-violet
green-blue and orange-red	green-blue and red-orange

A *paired complementary color scheme* includes two or more pairs of complements and/or their tints and shades. This type of color scheme is not employed deliberately to any extent, it is hard to apply in flower arrangement. When using three pairs of complements let one pair dominate and place the others in analogous order; the result might be called an analogous-complementary scheme. This scheme seems to include nearly the entire color wheel, therefore it suggests completeness. It is practically the same as a polychromatic scheme. When many hues are combined it is best to use light values.

A Split Complementary Color Scheme. This type of scheme consists of *one key color* combined with the two colors that adjoin its complement on the color wheel. This scheme makes a much more interesting combination than the direct complements; in fact, it is one of the best and the easiest of color schemes. It still has the balance of opposites but it is more subtle than a direct complementary scheme. Again the best results occur with one color dominating, with some intensities reduced, and with variation in the values. Two examples of split complementaries from the eighteen-hued color wheel are:

1. *Yellow*, blue-violet, red-violet
2. *Green*, violet-red, orange-red

In a flower arrangement with a split complementary scheme of

violet, green-yellow, and orange-yellow, use the violet for the largest area, if the plant material permits, because that is the quietest
hue.

A Triad Color Scheme. This combines the three colors that occur at the *points of an equilateral triangle* placed anywhere on the
color wheel. Any tints and/or shades of these three colors may
be used, thus allowing great freedom of color. In a triadic arrangement one color should greatly dominate in quantity, possibly com-
prising four-fifths of the entire composition, and it should usually
be subdued in intensity. Sometimes only very small amounts of the
other two colors are used. Several values of the dominating color
are desirable. Triadic colors are so unrelated to one another that
they are liable to make an explosive combination, unless carefully
controlled.

Some triads from the twelve or the eighteen-hue wheel are:

1. Yellow, blue, red (the primaries)
2. Green, violet, orange (the secondaries)
3. Yellow-green, blue-violet, red-orange (some tertiaries)

In a flower arrangement that combines green, violet, and orange
the easiest solution but not the finest would be to use green for the
largest area, including some pale green tints for relief. The secondary
area might well be a muted violet, with a pale orange for the smallest area, for orange is the most potent color, even when diluted.
Another triadic scheme consists of red-orange tritomas, blue-violet
asters, and yellow-green leaves. In making or judging triad schemes
in flower shows considerable leeway must be given in the correctness
of the hues. In fact, many persons think it a waste of time to
bother with triads, because it is hard to find plant materials that
are just the right colors.

A Polychromatic Color Scheme. This scheme requires the use
of four, five, or six colors that do not comprise an analogous scheme.
This scheme allows the most freedom of color of any of the standard schemes and is considered by some to be the most fun. One
color should dominate in a polychromatic scheme. For the best results, the scheme should be definitely warm or definitely cool. Pale
or subdued colors throughout are the most satisfactory.

The polychromatic scheme is desirable for home use, for it allows a combination of garden flowers which must be cut frequently to keep them blooming. A mixture of light colors that includes most of the spectrum may be arranged as follows: a soft orange dominant in quantity and centrally placed, yellow and yellow-green at one side, and pink and lavender on the other side.

THE ART PRINCIPLES APPLIED TO COLOR

The major art principles are *proportion, balance, rhythm,* and *dominance.* In flower arrangements the art principles apply to *color* and also to the other art elements: line, form, and texture. These principles have been explained thoroughly in another chapter. However, their application to color is briefly considered here. (In judging flower arrangements by point scoring, it is well to consider all possible aspects of color under the one item *color.* Therefore, in this book, the application of the art principles to color is presented under Color rather than under Art Principles.)

Proportion.   Half-and-half divisions are monotonous, thirds or other similar fractions are preferable. Some proportions to avoid are:

(1) equal amounts of different colors
(2) equal amounts of cool and warm colors
(3) equal amounts of weak and strong colors
(4) equal amounts of light and dark values

Some colorists prefer the following proportions of *light and dark colors* in flower arrangements: 60% light, 30% medium, 10% dark, however opinions differ. Arrangers agree that if three hues are combined, there should be most of one, less of another one, and least of the third one. *Intensity proportions* that are usually recommended are: 3 parts of a much-grayed color, to 2 parts of a medium-grayed color, to 1 part of an intense color.

Balance.   Good color balance depends on the proper distribution of *visual weight,* so that the two sides of an arrangement appear equally heavy in color. A law of area-balance states that a small brilliant area of color on one side of a vertical axis will balance a large area of neutralized color on the other side. Balance is also helped by (1) placing *dark colors low* and light ones high and on the edges, (2) placing *bright colors low* and weak ones high and on the edges. In actual practice there are many exceptions to these guides to balance.

Dominance. *One selected color* should have the most emphasis; it should be predominant in the whole arrangement. The *center of interest* should have special emphasis, showing the brightest colors and possibly the greatest value contrast.

Rhythm. Related movement in color is obtained by using a *gradation in values* in the dominant color, as in passing gradually from a standard violet to a medium violet, then to a lavender, and on to a pale lavender. The same violet colors can also carry a gradation in intensity. For example, the standard pure violet would be intense and the others gradually grayed until finally the pale lavender is almost a pale gray. A *gradation in hues* is rhythmic too; it is the same as an analogous color scheme, as in a sequence of red-violet, violet, blue-violet, violet-blue, and blue. These same hues could also be a gradation in values if each neighboring color were lighter than the next one. This would heighten the rhythm and consequent beauty.

PROBLEMS IN COLOR
(Suggestions from which to choose)

Students may use ordinary wax crayons, colored pencils, poster paint, or water colors for their quick sketches in color. The standard colors, red, orange, yellow, green, blue, and violet, with black and white, are needed in the medium that is used.

1. Make a quick color wheel of six sections using the *primary* colors with the secondary colors between them: r,o,y,g,b,v.
2. Make a quick color wheel of twelve sections using the *primary* and *secondary* colors and the *tertiary* colors that come between them: r,o-r,o,o-y,y,g-y,g,g-b,b,v-b,v,v-r.
3. Make a quick color wheel showing eighteen hues (see page 67).
4. Make a *value scale* of any hue or black showing six different values (see page 70).
5. Make a chart of six squares showing the three pure primary hues and

beside them the same hues that have been reduced *in intensity*. Add some of its complement to any color to reduce its intensity.

6. Make an arrangement using only *cool colors* (greens, blues, violets, white, gray, and black).
7. Make an arrangement using only *warm colors* (reds, oranges, yellows, cream, and brown).
8. Make a flower arrangement in an *analogous scheme* including green, yellow-green or green-yellow, and yellow (see page 85).
9. Make a *monochromatic* arrangement in brown and tan dry materials (see page 180).
10. Make a monochromatic foliage arrangement using some light values.
11. Make a flower arrangement using a complementary color scheme (see page 57).

A POLYCHROMATIC SCHEME

MONOCHROMATIC COLOR SCHEME. Branches of gray sage leaves, a gray pottery container, and roses in three different values of pink give a delicate color effect. The roses follow the line established by the branches, making a self-balanced, asymmetrical line arrangement. The addition of several silvery-green begonia leaves below the two bottom roses would change this to a line-mass arrangement in a complementary color scheme.

84

ANALOGOUS COLOR SCHEME. Pale green grapes, green dates, yellow-green horse-apples, yellow gourds, brass container, and orange pyracantha berries make up the color rhythm ranging from green to orange. While the long diagonal movement is dramatic, the opposing diagonal movement on the table is necessary for balance. Unimaginative judges in flower shows might not reward the arranger who dares to challenge gravity to this extent, but the composition would be suitable for a tea-party table at home or at a club.

THEME: CONTRASTS. Color contrast results from combining pale lavender chrysanthemums, chartreuse banana-tree stalks, and green pine. Distinctive texture contrasts are featured in these sleek, spiky, and feathery materials.

86

PART III

Expressiveness

Chapter 10

THEMES

One objective in making a flower arrangement is to make it beautiful; another objective is to make it *express a definite idea*. A beautiful arrangement that expresses some theme or character has more distinction than one that has only beauty, just as a beautiful woman with an interesting personality has more charm than one with beauty alone.

The word *expressiveness* means the quality of portraying or stating—in other words, *expressing*—something clearly. It means somewhat the same as character or personality, but it is a better art term than either of these words for it has in it less of the suggestion of human attributes. The word expression should not be substituted for expressiveness, for its meaning is not the same. Flower arrangers should adopt the word expressiveness for general use and also for their scales of points, because its precise meaning refers to the ability of an arrangement to express a theme or idea.

EXPRESSIVE ARRANGEMENTS

In flower arrangement, as in all the arts, the finished product should usually have expressiveness, it should carry a message of some kind. It may be cheer, dignity, humor, daintiness, or any other thought. The more definite the idea is, the more powerful and effective is the composition and the more pleasure it gives to observer and exhibitor. Thought association in relation to flower arrangement is a very old tradition, particularly in the Orient. Expert arrangers everywhere now realize that the spiritual quality of a flower arrangement is an important aspect of it.

Interpretative (or interpretive) arrangements are required in most of the arrangement classes in the advanced flower shows of today. In regular flower shows, also, some classes should have themes for interpretation. Some classes may specify a special setting or a special occasion that requires a flower arrangement to express a suitable mood. In all classes that name a theme, setting, or special occasion, *an idea* must be conveyed from the arranger to the observer. In flower-show competition an arranger should not timidly hint at the idea she is expressing; her work must shout it out or she will not be heard.

Expert arrangers usually prefer to make arrangements or compositions with themes. Those who have already learned to produce beauty will always find new unsolved problems to challenge their skill when they are called on to interpret ideas. As long as there are new ideas that appeal to the imagination, no arranger can ever feel that she has fully developed her art.

Even for home use it is good practice to *name your arrangement* before making it, and also to see if your family can guess from the finished arrangement what you were trying to say with your flowers. It is often easier to make a worthy arrangement when one is limited to a single theme or idea. Unless the arrangement says something positive it is not a significant achievement.

Personality. One's inner personality often is expressed in a flower arrangement. The design of an experimental modernist looks very different from that of a conservative person.

The outward moods and emotions of an arranger may also be expressed. For a gay mood, there are masses of light, bright, warm colors. For a serious mood, a sparse arrangement in blue and purples is consistent. An angry mood may bring out yucca spikes (daggers), and some red as a danger signal. A windy day may suggest a line arrangement that leans in the direction in which the wind is blowing. An arranger should feel intensely about an arrangement that she is making and then should try to transfer to others what she feels. To accomplish this she must be able to use the art elements and principles which are her tools.

The Art Elements. *Lines* can do much to help to express a definite mood or idea in flower arrangement. For example, curved lines express joy, radiating lines express liveliness, and diagonal lines express restless movement. In a theme named *Flight* an arranger might well feature diagonal lines.

Forms or shapes can also help to express specific ideas. The forms of the plant materials, container, base, accessories, and background all should promote the theme. The form of the complete arrangement is also expressive. Low, horizontal arrangements seem placid, while the vertical arrangements express aspiration and alertness. The curvilinear arrangements suggest grace and femininity. The theme *Her Royal Highness* might well be expressed in a Hogarth curve design of Talisman roses in a stately, slender golden urn. The theme *High Notes* would naturally be a tall vertical arrangement, with the most important flowers at the top.

Colors are also effective in suggesting emotional qualities: the warm colors are lively, the cool colors are quiet. Even color values are expressive, light colors are usually gay, dark ones are usually sober and dignified. Intense colors are bold, subdued colors are reserved. To express the themes *Welcome* or *Summer*, warm colors should be used; to express *Dawn*, pearly tints would be appropriate. Conflict of any kind could be best expressed through the opposition of complementary color schemes. The traditional symbolism of color is helpful to an arranger who is interpreting a theme in color; for this information see page 72.

Textures express ideas too. Rough textures seem masculine, strong, and sometimes rustic. Slick textures seem sophisticated and modern. Fine textures seem feminine and elegant. Many other effects can also be obtained through the use of appropriate textures. To express a theme in a flower arrangement it is usually necessary to have the textures all similar in effect. The theme *Miss Priss*, for a girl's bedroom bouquet, naturally suggests all fine textures.

The Art Principles. *Proportion is expressive.* Elongated things seem more elegant and fragile than short, thick masses. This is true in flower arrangement as well as in architecture and sculpture. *Scale* or size also influences ideas: small things suggest refinement, large things suggest strength and dominance. *Quantity* affects a mood too, sparse materials suggesting restraint and reflection, large amounts of materials suggesting exuberance and abundance.

Balance expresses dignity or formality if it is symmetrical, and subtlety or informality if it is asymmetrical. To express a theme like *March Wind* asymmetrical balance could be so exaggerated that the observer would have the feeling of leaning with a strong wind. The theme *Easter Morn* requires symmetrical balance to express solemnity and dignity.

Rhythm is movement, so it sets the tempo as well as the direction and the kind of activity to be expressed in a flower arrangement. When an arranger wishes to express speed she needs to know that the more nearly upright a diagonal line is the faster the movement. To reduce the speed of a line an arranger uses breaks, bends, or curves in it. Some themes call for regular repeated rhythm and others for free variable rhythm. In the theme *Waltz*, both types of rhythm may appear; the lines should be graceful, circular, and meandering, and the 1-2-3 beat might well be repeated here and there.

Dominance, or its opposite, subordination, can be utilized to express moods and ideas. For example, in a theme called *Uncertainty*, dominance should be minimized. This theme might be expressed by the absence of a dominant color or a dominant focal point. The engagement theme *The One and Only* should show extreme dominance of one particular blossom over all other materials.

Repetition is the most important principle in expressing a theme like *A Marching Song*. Transition would be featured in the *Ice Carnival* theme. *Variation* would be needed in a theme such as *Roadside Memories*.

Contrast would be the guiding principle in the theme *Rivals*. Absence of any contrast would be necessary in order to express *Boredom*.

Plant Materials. Specific ideas can be conveyed by the selection of certain plant materials. In general, flower arrangements should express energy, life, and animation, because that is what growing plant materials themselves express. Flowers are particularly expressive: they carry many messages of love, cheer, and consolation.

Garden flowers express quite different ideas from florists' flowers. One spray of flowers from the garden expresses the present season, the freshness of growing things, and often the personal devotion of a flower-lover and flower-grower. Some arrangers think that no florists' flowers should be added to an arrangement of garden flowers; however, where beauty is the objective, such combinations may be necessary.

Florists' flowers have their own range of expressiveness. Where gardens are dormant half the year, florists' flowers fill the human need for cheerful, living beauty. Arrangers must use imagination in order to introduce the play spirit into arrangements of florists' flowers. If possible, buds, half-blown, and full-blown flowers should be purchased together to express the continuity of growth. Out of a dozen flowers, three or five may be lighter or darker for use at the center of interest. A dozen large red roses, equally developed, with equally long stems placed in a tall container express affluence most of all. When the stems are all cut at different lengths, however, and the flowers are arranged with thought, beauty and expressiveness may result.

No doubt the most beautiful of all arrangements are those in which the spirit of the flower itself is expressed.

Foliage, as well as flowers, can express definite ideas in arrangements. The first tender green leaves on the trees are the very essence of spring. The colorful leaves of the maple or sumac are a dramatic message of autumn. Pine foliage is expressive of hills; wild iris foliage and some ferns are expressive of the swamps. Pepper tree foliage expresses delicacy and femininity, loquat tree foliage expresses strength and masculinity. Vines that hang downward are sad-looking; leaves that radiate like yucca spikes are alert and dangerous. The size, the form, the texture, and the color of leaves affect their expressiveness.

Dry materials express only the dormant winter to some persons. To others dry seed pods and nuts express the ideas of continuity of life and harvest time. Any dry plant materials that are interesting

CLASSIFICATION BY CHARACTERISTICS
OF FLOWERS

Formality *Dignity*	*Informality* *Modesty*	*Modernity*
Calla-lily	Bachelor Button	Amaryllis
Camellia	Calendula	Anthurium
Canterbury Bell	Cosmos	Banana blossom
Carnation	Daisy	Bird-of-Paradise
Chrysanthemum (large)	Gaillardia	Cactus
Delphinium	Geranium	Calla-lily
Foxglove	Marigold	Cereus
Gardenia	Narcissus	Cup of Gold
Gladiolus	Nasturtium	Foxglove
Iris	Pansy	Lotus
Lily	Petunia	Magnolia grandiflora
Lupine	Phlox	Oriental Poppy
Poinsettia	Scabiosa	Pitcher Plant
Rose	Snapdragon	Tiger Lily
Stock	Sunflower	Tritoma
Tulip	Sweet Pea	Water-lily
Zinnia (large)	Violet	Yucca

in form and texture can be organized to create beauty and express ideas just as living plant materials do. One entire show of dry materials had the appropriate theme *Brittle Beauty*.

Fruit and vegetable arrangements, like flower arrangements, are able to express specific ideas. Some Latin American countries express the abundance of their lush tropical vegetation in their large, mixed, colorful mass arrangements of fruits and flowers. The Japanese, on the other hand, express the sparseness of vegetation on their mountains and their small land areas in their tastefully restrained arrangements, sometimes made of a few pieces of fruit with foliage. In a flower show a fruit class entitled *Contrasts* might be expressed with a pineapple, sleek purple plums, and long spikes of sansevieria. A class named *Down to Earth* could be expressed in vegetables and succulents if the class specifications permitted.

Containers, too, are able to express certain ideas, even when empty. The materials of which they are made are expressive. Costly materials usually express elegance. Inexpensive pottery and wooden containers may suggest simplicity, strength, or ruggedness. Baskets express naturalness, directness, and lack of weight. Metal containers express strength, hardness, or permanence; silver, however, expresses elegance also. Glass usually expresses fragility, but thick glass suggests strength and bulk.

The forms of containers are expressive too, the tall ones being aspiring and the low ones solid and contented. Period containers express the same ideas as the other decorations of their day.

Accessories are so very expressive that many less able arrangers depend upon them to carry any message they wish to convey. Figurines of animals and human beings can be found to express many themes that appear in flower shows. The most skillful arrangers, however, usually prefer to suggest the theme through expressive plant materials and natural accessories. Rocks, fungi, driftwood, cones, shells, and plant materials fit best into flower or foliage arrangements because they are not man-made and have no connotations of artificiality.

SUGGESTIONS FOR FLOWER SHOW THEMES

The entire arrangement division of an advanced flower show usually has a theme, to unify the many otherwise unrelated exhibits. The theme also adds interest to the show for the public and the exhibitors. Some themes for the entire arrangement division of a flower show are: *Springtime in the Rockies, Autumn Festival, A Musical Program, United Nations, A Book of Verse, Seaside Sports, The Art Gallery, and Silver Jubilee.*

In this age of international disturbances garden clubs could add something to harmony and good will by having flower shows with themes honoring our neighbor nations and friends. *Canada, Cuba, Hawaii, Japan,* or *Mexico* are excellent general themes for the arrangement sections of flower shows in the United States. Flowers are sometimes flown in for the horticulture section too.

Canada. This theme would permit a varied, interesting show. The period styles of both England and France were brought to Canada by administrative officials and settlers; therefore many different period flower arrangements might be used in a flower show with a Canadian theme. The present-day industries, the modern projects, exploration, the Eskimo, and Canadian plant materials provide fascinating themes for interpretive arrangements, especially in our northern states.

Cuba. Cuba's exciting history, her wonderful plant materials, and her ocean life provide a great variety of themes for an entire flower show. A class of arrangements suggesting Murillo or Picasso would have interesting possibilities. The period arrangements of Spain would strongly contrast with something the natives might have used in pre-Columbian days. A class with live tropical fish would not be impossible, while the beautiful shells would be choice containers.

Hawaii. Native good taste, happy leisure time, Oriental influence, and beautiful plant materials have helped to make Hawaii the land-of-no-poor-flower-arrangements. Nowhere in Honolulu, in restaurants, stores, or homes, does one see careless or ugly handling of flowers; therefore Hawaii deserves to be the theme of many flower shows. What an array of titles for various classes comes to mind! Just to illustrate the songs and the various hula dances would be an achievement. The symbolic creations of the Buddhist priests, the subtle beauty of the work of the Japanese flower arrangement teachers, the stunning work of Caroline Peterson at the Academy of Art, and the polished arrangements by the garden club members should inspire a variety of themes and titles.

Japan. What better theme could a flower show have than to honor the first nation to create enduring classical flower arrangements? The exhibitors in a show that had a Japanese theme would gain much from the intensive study that would be necessary for most of them. An educational display of the work of a Japanese arranger would be most helpful.

Mexico. That stimulating theme, *Mexico*, has often been used in American flower shows because many Americans are acquainted with Mexican life and flowers. This theme produces a beautiful varied show because classes may portray the *native art and customs,* the early imported European *period styles,* and the beautiful *modern style.* The decorative use of their abundant flowers, foliage, and fruit has been an important part of Mexican life, from the earliest days to the present. Flower arrangement is therefore of great significance in homes, churches, and other public meeting places, as well as in the beautiful flower shows presented by the garden clubs in some cities of Mexico.

A Successful Theme. A few years ago the author was arrangement schedule chairman of the Louisiana State Flower Show that won the top award in the nation from the National Council of State Garden Clubs. The theme chosen for the arrangement section was *Southern Hospitality.* All the themes selected for the different classes were appropriate under the general theme. Some of the classes were *Welcome Stranger,* (for the hall table), *Mint Julep,* (green and white), *Future Hospitality,* (ultra-modern), *Jazz, Born in Dixie,* (a line arrangement), *Party Manners,* (a Victorian arrangement, in a niche), *Joie de Vivre,* (a Louis XVI adaptation in a niche), *Function and Fun,* (a modern buffet table), and *Tarpon Rodeo,* (an outdoor table with a seashore motif). The unity resulting from the one theme was an important factor in winning the National award.

THEMES FOR FLOWER ARRANGEMENTS

VARIETY IS THE SPICE OF LIFE. Spice cans as accessories.

ALL THAT GLITTERS IS NOT GOLD. Gilded fruit and foliage.

GARDEN CLUBBERS. Big white hen and small white bird and foliage.

SIDEWALK CAFE. Dry materials and lobster claws.

HAWAIIAN MEMORY. Fern and piece of fine white coral.

STAFF OF LIFE. Bundles of wheat on straws with rolled corn husk flowers.

YOUNG AUDACITY. Cut aspidistra leaves with stem end up. One big flower made of croton leaves.

IN THE BEGINNING. Landscape with pond, foliage, grasses, and ceramic lizards.

NATURE'S RUFFLES. Parsley, petunias, or other ruffled materials.

SOMETHING OLD AND SOMETHING NEW. Dry twig and flowers.

CHRYSANTHEMUM CASCADE. Waterfall effect in tall vase, using white flowers.

HINT OF SPRING. Dry material dominant with a bit of green and a flower.

FLOWER MOSAIC. Small flowers in patterns in a flat arrangement.

RING AROUND A ROSY. Paper lace circle and flowers around a rose.

APRIL FOOL. Simulated flowers made from vegetables.

GAY DECEIVERS. Flowers made from leaves (painted or not).

NEWLY BORN. An opening date palm sheath.

THE NEW LOOK. Anthurium or other streamlined materials.

A BIT OF BOGLAND. A naturalistic landscape composition.

INDIAN SUMMER. Warm colors in leaves and seed pods.

FAREWELL TO ARMS. The Peace rose with buds.

OLD FAITHFUL. One stalk of white crinum or amaryllis flowers.

THE LONESOME PINE. One pine branch shaped like a tree.

CHINATOWN. A sparse arrangement in Chinese container with figurines.

EBB TIDE. Interesting things found on the beach.

RHAPSODY IN BLUE. Blue container with delicate blue and silver materials.

THE BIRD WALK. Roadside materials, pottery birds for accessories.

EASTER PARADE. Arrangement suggesting an Easter bonnet.

INDEPENDENCE DAY. Patriotic theme. A triangular arrangement. Blue delphinium at top and extending diagonally to lower left side. Row of white stock below the blue delphinium. White candytuft at the lower right side. One dozen red carnations for the focal point.

MODERN ART. In the spirit of Salvador Dali. A modern flower arrangement using tulips, calla-lilies, and gladioli, with aspidistra leaves cut off diagonally. The vase is a pair of sun-tanned hands.

THE SPIRIT OF SPRING. A vertical arrangement. Yellow, yellow-green, and white suggest the new season. Vertical lines of foliage and flowers produce a sprightly, upspringing effect. In a chartreuse

container use white and yellow narcissi with their own leaves and
some ginger lily leaves.

STAG SUPPER. A line and mass arrangement. Humorous. Small
bunches of cigarettes on the ends of long wires, with red geraniums
and green and white rubber-plant leaves at the base, in a low red
bowl.

Easter	Daintiness	Angel's Wings
Fourth of July	Drama	Break a Rule
Thanksgiving	Dignity	Candid Camera
Horn of Plenty	Elegance	Essence
Christmas	Humor	Field Day
Church	Luxury	Fuchsia Falls
Jewels	Primness	Glad Summer
Music	Refinement	Hi-Jinks
Wonderland	Restraint	Ideas of March
Childhood	Simplicity	Mardi-Gras
Wind	Sturdiness	New Leaves
Rain	Thrift	Noah's Ark
Georgia O'Keefe	Quaintness	Peace and Joy
Surrealism	Femininity	Peace and Plenty
Argentine Art	Swamp Beauty	Plantation Melody
Brazilian Beauty	Deep South	Rhapsody in Blue
Canadian Coolness	Mountain Side	Rococo
Cuban Rhumba	Woods Plunder	Sea Symphony
Hawaii Calls	Roadside	Table Talk
Japanese Guest	Drifted In	This is my Best
Mexican Music	Beach Combings	Treasure Chest
January Junk	September Silks	Spring Song
February Findings	October Ode	Spring Spectacle
March Mysteries	November Night	Summer Siesta
April Architecture	December Delights	Summer Splendor
May Midgets	Morning Mist	Autumn Aristocrats
June Jewels	Noon Note	Autumn Allergies
July Jade	Night Nuance	Winter Winds
August Attractions	Day Dreams	Winter Welcome

Study of Paintings. Students of flower arrangement would do
well to study mood and theme in paintings. Notice how misty morning effects are obtained by neutralized colors in very close values.

Observe how gaiety is warm, brilliant, and contrasty in color, and diagonal, vertical, or circular in line. See how peace is expressed with cool reflective hues in sober values, and with restful horizontals, aided perhaps by a rising line of hope and gratitude. An arranger should notice which pictures express a definite mood, and try to realize how the artist created this mood. Then he or she might consider the possibility of obtaining such a mood in a flower arrangement, through the medium of container and plant materials. As in painting, the fusion of expressiveness and beauty is necessary to produce the best results.

PROBLEMS IN EXPRESSIVENESS
(Suggestions from which to choose)

1. Draw lines and forms that seem to express an idea or emotion.
2. Make an arrangement expressing the theme *Youth*.
3. Make an arrangement expressing the theme *Spring, Summer, Fall,* or *Winter* (see page 138).
4. Make an arrangement that expresses *Masculine Qualities* (see page 139).
5. Make an arrangement that expresses *Femininity* (see page 160).
6. Make an arrangement that expresses *The Family,* both Man and Woman.
7. Make an arrangement that expresses the personality of some well-known actress.
8. Make an arrangement that expresses your own personality.
9. Make an arrangement that suggests a Disney character or episode (see page 101).
10. Make an arrangement wherein the colors express a mood or idea.

THEME: THE SORCERESS. The mood of black magic is expressed by the Oriental dancer, the tall caladium bud and the flame-like paper-plant leaves.

THEME: A DISNEY EPISODE. The caladium serpent has defeated the palm leaf eagle.

A NEOCLASSIC ADAPTATION, Louis XVI, Late Georgian (Adam), or Federal U.S.A. (Post-Revolutionary). This arrangement is feminine, symmetrical, small in size though relatively tall, slender, pale in color, delicate in texture, restrained and well designed. The marble slab suggests Pompeii, where the excavations started the Neoclassic style.

PART IV

Occidental and Oriental Styles

Period Flower Arrangements
Japanese Flower Arrangements

Chapter 11

PERIOD FLOWER ARRANGEMENTS

Traditional occidental flower arrangements are commonly known as "period" arrangements, and are a minor part of the three great decorative movements of Europe. These decorative movements are the *Renaissance* (1400–1600), the *Baroque* (1600–1775) (including the *Rococo*), and the *Neoclassic* (1775–1830). All of these except the Rococo started in Italy and spread over Europe and finally to America. Their decorative styles affected every art expression, from architecture and furnishings to floral decoration. In this book we consider only those period flower arrangements most likely to be useful to arrangers of today in their homes, churches, clubs, and flower shows.

THE RENAISSANCE PERIOD (1400–1600)

Italian Renaissance. This style, developed in Italy, was mostly a rebirth of the classical style of Greece and Rome. It influenced all the life and products of this art-conscious age. The work of the Della Robbia brothers is especially interesting to flower arrangers; their terra cotta wreaths and frames of flowers, leaves, fruit, and nut motifs are inspiring models. The paintings of Botticelli, Raphael, and other old masters show the garlands, wreaths, and flower arrangements of this period.

Most Renaissance flower arrangements were large, tall, symmetrical, and pyramidal in form. They were open, airy, and uncrowded; the containers were often about the same height as the plant materials. Some low compositions of flowers and fruit in low containers also appeared in the details of paintings. Arrangements were also made in cornucopias for carrying in parades. Bright, contrasting colors were the fashion, and triad color schemes were the most popular of all.

Favorite containers were classic wide-mouthed marble urns, and pedestal vases of metal; but red Venetian glass vases, and pottery jugs, bowls, drug jars, and bowls with stems, called *tasses*, were also used.

An *adaptation* of a Renaissance flower arrangement would be suitable today for church or stage or for a formal tea table. It might be given extra dignity by the addition of several marble bases. Many plant materials that are common today were used in the Renaissance period, so there are plenty of flowers that are authentic. Some favorites were lilies, roses, violets, jasmine, pinks, lilies-of-the-valley, daisies, irises, anemones, primroses, and carnations, with laurel, olive, or ivy leaves for contrast. No hybrids should be used in this period arrangement. If background fabrics are employed they may be velvet, brocade, damask, or cloth of gold, plain or small-patterned. Crimson, gold, green, and blue were favorite colors in fabrics.

Other countries copied the Italian Renaissance style. France adopted it and developed her own interpretation of it. Spain absorbed it during the period of her highest achievement, and combined it with Moorish influence. England, too, had its Renaissance, but it was not as fine as the continental.

Colonial United States received two versions of the Renaissance, the Early American of the eastern coast and the Spanish Colonial of the Southwest. Naturally these were simplified interpretations that were very unlike the original Renaissance style.

Early American, Early Colonial, or Pilgrim Century Period (1620–1720). A transition style of the late English Renaissance (Jacobean), sometimes called Cromwellian, was brought to America by the humble, religious Puritans who were mostly from the rural middle class in England. Their religion required simplicity and restraint in everything, including color and decoration. We can assume that any flower arrangements made in this earliest American period were natural, casual, simple, and frequently small because their rooms were small.

An *adaptation* of an Early American arrangement might well have a background of natural pine wood or stained wood. The container should be simple; in fact almost any worn pioneer-type utensil would convey the desired mood. Handwoven fabrics and table carpets would be fitting. Solidity, naturalness, and humility are ideas to express in Early American arrangements.

The Spanish Colonial Style.   In the sixteenth century Spanish priests and soldiers introduced to our southwestern area a crude and simplified version of the Spanish Renaissance and Baroque styles. This was influenced also by Mexican and Indian design and labor, and by crude tools and materials.

Today, *adaptations* of large imposing Spanish Renaissance flower arrangements might be made for special occasions, but in general the most suitable traditional arrangements of the Southwest would be influenced by the scarcity of plant materials, especially during the dry season. The yucca flower stalk (Our Lady's candle), which grows in the desert, is dramatic and suitable for church arrangements. The containers for Spanish Colonial arrangements may be Spanish, Mexican, or Indian receptacles made of pottery, stone, metal, wood, or basketry. Any fabrics used should be indigenous. Leather would be appropriate underneath some arrangements. Accessories of special interest are available that are true to the traditional Spanish Colonial style.

THE BAROQUE PERIOD (1600–1775)

Italy.   The Baroque movement was a reaction and a rebellion against the classical Renaissance style; it was inspired and led by the great artist Michelangelo. The many paintings of this period show us that flower decorations expressed the exuberant mood of the Baroque. The flower arrangements were very large, lush, and abundant, showing combinations of many kinds of flowers and fruits, some very large, some small.

Symmetrical arrangements were used early in the Baroque period, especially in tall urns in the gardens, as shown in many tapestries. But symmetry was discarded, along with the other restraints of the Renaissance.

Asymmetrical curves, especially large low S curves and arching stopped C curves, predominated in typical Baroque flower arrangements. Usually the dominant movement started low down on one side and swept upward to the top of the other side, often in a strong curved diagonal. Many other minor movements made every spot on the arrangement exciting and gay. Sometimes several centers of interest were in competition. The total effect was dynamic and moving, but always graceful.

Color was unrestrained in the Baroque period arrangements. Usually they were colorful, mostly warm, of medium values, but with enough lights for sparkle. The arrangements were placed against cool green, blue, purple, or gray backgrounds for contrast.

Textures were varied and exquisite in flowers, fruits, and fabrics. Velvets, damasks, brocades, taffetas, and Oriental fabrics were often used as backgrounds.

Containers were always large, sometimes enormous. They were made of sturdy materials, such as metals, stone, pottery, and heavy glass. Some Oriental porcelains were also used. Round and oval urn shapes, pedestal vases, jugs, flasks, jars, and bowls were favored for flowers; low baskets were popular for fruit arrangements.

Plant materials in great variety were used in the Baroque period. Large variegated flowers were favorites. Cyclamen, carnations, anemones, peonies, tulips, datura, foxglove, hollyhock, larkspur, lupine, narcissus, roses, lilies, and many others were used. Bold leaves like those of acanthus, canna, peony, and grape added strength to flower arrangements. Fruit was freely used by itself and in compositions with leaves and flowers.

Holland and Flanders (Belgium). (1600–1750). In the Low Countries the painting of flower pieces was very important and reached its height in the second half of the seventeenth century. Merchant princes commissioned the leading artists to paint huge and handsome arrangements of their flowers with horticultural accuracy.

Among the earliest Flemish painters were Jan Brueghel and Ambrosius Bosschaert, who often painted details for Rubens' pictures. They were followed by Roelant Saverij, Daniel Seghers, and Jan D. Heem.

Some of the best Dutch painters of flower pieces were Abraham van Beyeren, William van Aelst, and Jan van Huysum, but the greatest of all the flower painters of the Low Countries was a woman, Rachel Ruysch. Many other Dutchwomen were also flower painters of distinction, and their work can be seen in the museums.

Flower arrangements of the Lowlands (Holland and Flanders) were the largest and most compact of all arrangements. They had much variety, but some characteristics were general. The proportions were better than those of the Italian Baroque arrangements. The flower materials were taller in relation to the containers, which were rather small and inconspicuous. The beloved tulips were prominent in most of the arrangements, usually combined with many other kinds of flowers. Entertaining accessories appeared in the flower pictures: birds, birds' nests, butterflies, insects, shells, watches, and jewelry. The earliest arrangements were fairly symmetrical, but this effect was later replaced by Baroque curves and asymmetrical movement.

Adaptations of these arrangements, that portray the mood of this period, would be suitable in homes that have Dutch, English, or Spanish Baroque furnishings and in those flower shows in which space is not limited.

France. In the French Baroque period the court of Louis XIV was the most brilliant in Europe. His palace and gardens at Versailles were magnificent. The king commissioned Nicolas Robert and Jean-Baptiste Monnoyer to paint pictures of flower arrangements. The artist Charles le Brun was also one of the flower arrangers of the court. French Baroque flower arrangements had the same general characteristics as the Italian, but were somewhat lighter in color and more airy. The containers were large and handsome, and were in scale with the arrangements.

An *adaptation* of a Louis XIV arrangement would be suitable in a hotel lobby or some other large room, especially with Baroque furniture. It should be impressive, bold, and masculine, but it should also have grace.

Spain (1650–1775). The Baroque influence came to Spain first from Italy and later from France and Flanders. Some Spanish artists painted masterful compositions of flower arrangements with horticultural accuracy. Among them were Juan de Arellano and Francesco de Zurbarán. Velasquez painted a charming flower arrangement in one of his portraits of the Infanta Margareta Theresa.

Adaptations of Spanish Baroque arrangements should have the richness of form, the contrasts of texture, and the riot of colors that suggest their Spanish background. They might well include Moorish containers and tiles. In a flower show the front of a niche for a flower arrangement might be made in the shape of the typical horseshoe arch.

England. The Baroque period occurred during the reigns of Queen Anne, George I, and George II, so it is often called Early Georgian. The Baroque style had spread from Italy through France and the Low Countries to England. One leading exponent of the style was Thomas Chippendale, a master cabinet maker. An English nurseryman, Robert Furber, published Peter Casteel's (Flemish) *Flowers of the Months*, and also his fruit compositions. Jacob van Huysum's (Dutch) *Flower Calendar* was also published in England. Grinling Gibbons, an Englishman, designed and carved in wood many beautiful swags of fruit and flowers that ornamented fireplaces and walls.

An *adaptation* of an Early Georgian arrangement should have the breadth, fullness, and richness of the French, Dutch, and Italian examples of Baroque. These arrangements were the progenitors of the American Colonial arrangements. Chinese containers and accessories are suitable in this period, especially with Chinese Chippendale furniture and with any Oriental furniture and rugs that suggest the period.

American Colonies (United States). The Baroque or Colonial period (1720–1780) is well illustrated at Williamsburg, Virginia. Louise B. Fisher's book, *An Eighteenth-Century Garland*, presents flower and fruit arrangements similar to those that decorate the restored buildings of Colonial Williamsburg. It is safe to assume that the colonists of this period copied the English flower arrangements, since they copied English furnishings and architecture. Furber's prints and other English flower prints were well known in the colonies.

American Colonial arrangements were probably somewhat less profuse than English arrangements because flowers were scarcer in the colonies; however, broad, full-bodied compositions in wide-mouthed, stemmed bowls are considered typical of the Colonial period. In winter these arrangements were often made of dry materials. Fruits were also freely used for decoration, especially on dining-room tables. Containers were made of silver, pottery, porcelain, stoneware, or basket fibers.

An *adaptation* of a Colonial flower arrangement should repeat the characteristics listed earlier under the general heading of Baroque. It should be large, broad, and usually somewhat asymmetrical, possibly with a hint of the S curve. It should express boldness, exuberance, excitement, and abundance through its size, form, and color. A lush colonial arrangement may consist of flowers, leaves, and fruit. The container should be large and strong; any fabrics should be heavy and elegant.

THE ROCOCO STYLE

France.   The Rococo Period of Louis XV (1715–1774) is a completely French variation of the Baroque style. The Rococo spread to rural France and became the most important Provincial influence. It also spread to most of Europe, and to the Americas. However, it was of less importance than the other decorative movements considered here.

In the Rococo (rock and shell) period all art forms became asymmetrical and entirely curvilinear; the lighter C curves took the place of the S curves. The Rococo style expressed femininity, gaiety, playfulness, and charm.

Flower arrangements of the Rococo period were portrayed in tapestries, fabrics, flower prints, and paintings. In the arrangements the plant materials were often about the height of the containers, but proportions varied. A few large flowers were used, but many small flowers and sprays, vines, or ferns made the arrangements airy. Many small bouquets were used on small tables. The colors were lighter, rosier, and more subtle than the Baroque, and the textures were finer.

Rococo *containers* were usually wide-mouthed, as urns, epergnes, basket shapes, Chinese bowls, shells, porcelain shells, tall vases, and flasks. The favorite accessories were the Rococo figurines made in the many ceramic factories, as in Dresden and Meissen.

An *adaptation* of a French Rococo arrangement should be a delicate, curvaceous composition in pale colors. An asymmetrical container would be suitable. A playful, feminine, whimsical, joyous mood should be expressed.

THE NEOCLASSICAL PERIOD (1775–1830)

Italy. *The Classical Revival, or Neoclassical* movement was inspired by the discovery of the buried cities of Pompeii and Herculaneum. Greek and Roman classicism replaced the Baroque style in buildings, interiors, and furnishings, in much of Europe. *Straight lines* and *symmetrical balance* took the place of asymmetrical curves.

Flower arrangements, garlands, and *swags* of the period were pictured in wall panels, tapestries, brocades, and paintings. The arrangements were symmetrical but they were fairly small, tall, slender, and airy. They were elegant in texture. They were often very restricted in color: grayed hues and light values were preferred, cool colors were predominant.

Neoclassical arrangements had many characteristics of the best compositions of the present. They usually had a dominant center of interest, and they had transition from denseness at the center to sparseness at the edges, as well as transition from large forms at the center to small ones at the top and sides.

Containers were varied in form. Greek and Roman shapes were most popular, including oval or boat-shaped bowls like Greek lamps. Alabaster, marble, opaque glass, silver, bronze, painted tin (tole), and fine ceramics, especially lusterware, were all used for containers.

Plant materials were greatly varied too, but the favorites of the ancients were featured: laurel, ivy, and oak leaves, grains, pomegranates, figs, quinces, roses, anemones, and flowering bulbs.

England. The Neoclassical Period or the Late Georgian (1759–1830) was mostly the product of the architect Robert Adam. Sheraton and Hepplewhite designed furniture in the same tradition. Angela Kaufman painted classical baskets of flowers and garlands for wall decorations at this time.

The flower arrangements in England were like the other Neoclassical arrangements, tall, slender, symmetrical, pale, cool, and elegant. *The containers* had distinction. The potter Josiah Wedgwood made classical forms and finished them with beautiful lusters. Tall slender urns, oval, elliptical, or boat-shaped footed containers, and baskets were favored.

France.   Louis XVI (1774–1842) reigned during the Neoclassical period. Typical flower arrangements in this style may be seen in tapestries, textiles, wall panels, and pictures. James Neilson designed fine flower arrangement motifs for tapestries for the French court.

An *adaptation* of a French classical arrangement for use today should be like the English and Italian arrangements but smaller and lighter in color. It, too, should be tall, slender, and symmetrical, and should express femininity, delicacy, and elegance. It should employ rather small plant materials such as anemones, bachelor buttons, camellias, lilies-of-the-valley, violas, and precise ferns. A small, plain, white alabaster urn would be a typical container for this period. Any fabrics used should be elegant but not heavy. Striped fabrics were very popular. Arrangements of this style are useful today in almost any small apartment or home where traditional furniture is used.

United States.   The Neoclassical, Federal, or Post-Revolutionary period (1790–1820) has the same characteristics as the European Neoclassical. The French influence, however, was stronger than the English after the war.

An *adaptation* of an American Federal period flower arrangement would be like a Louis XVI arrangement: delicate, pale, cool, tall, slender, airy, and symmetrical, in a tall, slender urn or a footed oval bowl. In the new Republic patriotic motifs were used in most of the accessories.

THE EMPIRE STYLE

France: Napoleon. (1804–1814). The Classical Revival includes the Empire style, but this is so very different from the chief style of the Neoclassical period that it is considered separately here. Two architects, Percier and Fontaine, developed the Empire style, which was masculine, pompous, militaristic, dramatic, large, and heavy. Roman and Egyptian motifs were used freely. An artist of the period, Pierre-Joseph Redouté, was a famous painter of flowers. Another artist, Jean-Louis Prévost, painted flower arrangements that expressed the weight of the Empire style, but with gracefully tapering tops. Large, pyramidal flower arrangements in broad Roman urns on tall pedestals were generally used; foliage such as laurel made backgrounds for masses of large red roses or peonies. Large garlands and wreaths were also used for decoration. The colors employed were strong, dark, and contrasting. Textures too were varied and bold, but rich.

England. The English version of the Empire style is the Regency (George IV) style; the floral decorations of that period were about the same as those of the French Empire, but lighter in weight.

United States. The American Empire style in furnishings was like the French, but was somewhat lighter in weight and more graceful. Duncan Phyfe made beautiful furniture in this style. American flower arrangements too were no doubt somewhat lighter and smaller than the original Empire arrangements.

An *adaptation* of an American Empire flower arrangement would probably be a large one in a heavy urn, that might even be draped with garlands. It might stand on a marble-topped table or on a tall pedestal. An asymmetrical adaptation of medium size might be made in a sled-shaped container or a metal basin. Other possibilities are a thick crescent in a marble cornucopia or a garland of flowers hung from the handles of a handsome covered urn. The abundant flowers should be large, showy, and rich in color. A typical arrangement might contain roses, peonies, irises, cycad leaves, and fruits. Black or dark green marble bases would help to express the masculine Empire mood.

THE NINETEENTH CENTURY (1820–1900)

France. In the nineteenth century France produced the best flower painters of the West. They brought originality and vitality to the arts of flower arrangement and flower painting. They had no general style; each artist expressed himself in his own way, and stands as a valuable example for arrangers of today who fear to experiment. Prints of these fine French paintings should adorn the homes of progressive flower arrangers.

Pierre Bonnard painted sunny tables with baskets of fruit and pitchers of flowers in fine harmonious colors; *Paul Cézanne*, the father of Post-impressionism, painted advanced, structural compositions of fruit, flowers, and accessories with unsurpassed ability. *Ann Vallayer-Coster* painted plump, balanced arrangements that were copied in Gobelin tapestries. *Gustave Courbet* painted casual arrangements of his favorite flowers, roses. *Hilaire Dégas* showed beautiful bouquets in the hands of his dancers. *Eugène Delacroix* painted casual arrangements of great beauty. *Eduard Manet*, leader of the Impressionists, painted beautiful flower arrangements with a loose, free technique. *Paul Gauguin* painted decorative, colorful, exotic flower arrangements that expressed the primitive life in Tahiti. *Henri Matisse* painted rather simple flower arrangements placed in his typical, highly decorative, gayly patterned interiors. *Odillon Redon* painted flower arrangements that were formless, but colorful, poetic, and expressive. *Auguste Renoir* painted beautiful, curved mass flower arrangements, with the same tenderness and skill he used in his figure painting. *Henri Rousseau* painted delightful stylized flower arrangements in his naive but very decorative manner. *Suzanne Valadon*, mother of Utrillo, painted strong, colorful, third-dimensional flower arrangements in harmonious colors. *Vincent van Gogh,*

Dutch genius who lived in France, painted stunning arrangements, especially of sunflowers, that could well serve as models for flower arrangers. In flower shows of today arrangements reminiscent of the work of any of the great painters mentioned above would be valuable exhibits.

England. The English Nineteenth Century or Victorian period is generally considered to be one of poor taste. No definite style prevailed but many were copied and combined. Certain characteristics of this romantic era, however, stand out with emphasis on a definite fashion, if not a style.

Victorian floral compositions were different from those on the continent at the same time. The English made arrangements of shell flowers, and wax flowers, and dried materials with skeletonized leaves, which they considered so precious that they were placed under glass domes for protection. Living flowers too were important in this period. The "language of flowers" was then in common social usage. The flower arrangements were opulent and fine-textured, and had the effect of all-over decorations. They were not well proportioned, being usually wider than high. They were very compact so that the effect was often stuffy and airless.

Asymmetrical balance was preferred to symmetrical in Victorian arrangements. White arrangements were popular for a time. Most arrangements were predominately cool in color with emphasis on rich purples and magentas; the variety in values made the whole effect spotty. There were usually several centers of interest, so that an arrangement was not unified in design.

Godey's Lady's Book, Harper's Weekly, and Currier and Ives prints show another type of Victorian arrangement—a casual, feathery, and sparse composition that displays the natural lines of a few flowers. In this type of arrangement moods were expressed, as bleeding hearts for love and droopy fuchsias for tears. Another type was the *tussy-mussy,* a small fragrant nosegay made in concentric circles and often carried in the hand.

The *plant materials* of the Victorian era are far too numerous to mention here. The arrangers preferred rich velvety textures, and sharp color contrasts. They especially liked flowers of variegated effects, such as streaked tulips, speckled lilies, splashy camellias, big-eyed anemones, bicolored pansies, and odd pelargoniums. Novel shapes were sought, too, such as the foxglove, bleeding heart, passion flower, cockscomb, and fuchsia. Large solid flowers like roses, dahlias, and peonies were favorites. Ferns, baby's breath, and heather were used for filler. They also used many dried flowers and leaves. Fruit was not used in Victorian flower arrangements.

Containers of the Victorian period were of many shapes and materials. Baroque, Rococo, and Neoclassical shapes were made in ceramics. Colored glass vases and bowls, brass and copper wine coolers, cast iron urns, alabaster urns, Oriental bowls, bottles, jars, silver cake baskets, trumpet epergnes of ceramics and silver, ceramic hands holding cornucopias, and pottery wall pockets were all used. Some were lavishly decorated and gilded.

The United States. The American Victorian era (1820–1900) was like the English Victorian. In most of the country our great-grandmothers had about the same kind of home furnishings, containers, and plant materials as the English women had.

An *adaptation* of a Victorian arrangement for a flower show today should maintain the mood of the original period, but the container may well be plain, the proportions pleasing, and the emphasis on one center of interest.

Further Study. A student of period arrangements should read at least three books on the subject: *Period Flower Arrangement* by Margaret F. Marcus, *Outlines of Period Flower Arrangement* by Frances J. Hannay, and *The Flower Piece in European Painting* by members of the staff of the Metropolitan Museum of Art in New York City. The book *Home Furnishing* by the present author has a condensed summary of period furnishings. In addition, the period arranger should visit if possible the American Wing and other period rooms at the Metropolitan Museum of Art, and authentic period rooms in other museums, as well as restored authentic dwellings.

PROBLEMS IN PERIOD ARRANGEMENTS
(Suggestions from which to choose)

1. Make a casual arrangement of simple materials in a simple container suggestive of the *Early American* period (Pilgrim century).
2. Make a large mixed mass arrangement to suggest the *Colonial* (pre-Revolutionary) period. Use any available flowers and containers, but try to express the mood of Williamsburg (see page 210).
3. Make a slender mass arrangement in a white urn in the *Federal* style (post-Revolutionary, Neoclassical) to suit the period of Mount Vernon and the Sheraton, Hepplewhite, and Adam furniture of the time.
4. Make a mixed mass arrangement, broad and buxom and influenced by the *Victorian* style (see page 119).
5. Keep your scrapbook of pictures of flower arrangements up to date. Classify them under headings like the chapters in this book.

AN EARLY AMERICAN SUGGESTION

BAROQUE ADAPTATION. Many characteristics of the original style are found in this very free interpretation of the Italian or Louis XIV manner. It is large, masculine, strong in color, rich in texture, and contains vigorous curves. The leaves make a long C curve. The dark alabaster container is correct in form. The flowers are not necessarily authentic, but are rather some of the usual garden flowers of autumn: roses, dahlias, chrysanthemums, with ligustrum (privet) berries and camellia leaves. The aim here is to express some of the exuberance of the first and greatest of the Baroque artists, Michelangelo.

VICTORIAN ADAPTATION. The confusion of many influences is apparent; the mood of the original period is approached by making the arrangement profuse and over-patterned like a Victorian room. There is no restraint or organization of the plant materials; they are scattered in an unrelated way with the largest next to the smallest and with several competing centers of interest. The flower mass is broader than it is tall. The flowers are those found in midsummer in an average garden, just as they would have been in the Victorian era. The container is authentic in form, but of recent make.

Chapter 12

JAPANESE FLOWER ARRANGEMENT

In Japan flower arrangement began about 550 A.D., when Buddhist priests decreed that flowers for temple use must be thoughtfully arranged to express some philosophic idea. The arrangements were often symbolic of the belief that love of flowers helps to harmonize man and nature, matter and spirit.

The first school of flower arrangement, Ikenobo, was established in the seventh century and is still in its original location at Rokkakudo temple in Kyoto. Ikenobo is the basis for a great many other schools that have developed in Japan. In the city of Tokyo alone there are now at least fifty flower arrangement schools accredited by the Board of Education and many hundreds of teachers of flower arrangement. Nearly all young Japanese women must study flower arrangement, for this accomplishment is considered a necessity, not a luxury.

The four main styles that have developed in Japanese flower arrangement are presented in this chapter; there are, however, a great many variations and subdivisions of these styles.

Rikka or *Rikkwa* began about 550 A.D. and was dominant until 1200. *Seika* or *Seikwa*, also called the Classical style, was begun about 1450 A.D. *Nageire* originated about 1600. *Moribana* was created shortly before 1900.

All these styles, except Rikka, have the basic Japanese *asymmetrical triangular design* with the three points or parts known as

120

Heaven, Man, and Earth. Modern Japanese teachers of flower arrangement use other terms for the three main lines. Some call them Primary (Heaven), Secondary (Man), and Tertiary (Earth), or Subject, Secondary and Object. The relative position of these three main lines, usually an irregular triangle, depends on the plant material and container used in the arrangement.

Asymmetrical balance is a feature of all styles of Japanese flower arrangements, except the earliest, the Rikka. Some Japanese arrangers explain this off-side balance by saying that it was a custom to place an arrangement against a wall near a window so that the lines of the arrangement pointed toward the light, the space between the arrangement and the window was a part of the design, and the window frame stopped the movement of the lines of the arrangement. In a Japanese home of today the arrangement often points to a related picture or to some other object of beauty that is placed near it.

Japanese arrangements are *one-front* (front-faced) compositions; the viewer should face the arrangement as the arranger did. The flowers are usually placed so as to face forward. Since flowers turn their best side to the sun, some arrangers consider themselves in the position of the sun and turn the flowers to face themselves.

Japanese arrangements have *three dimensions*. Depth is obtained by having the Heaven line upright and the Man and Earth lines leaning forward so that the tips make a triangle when seen from above. The Earth line, which protrudes the most, is considered to be the host part of a design, like a welcoming hand reaching forward to meet the guest.

All Japanese arrangements are either right- or left-handed. A *right-handed arrangement* is one in which the Heaven line and the Earth line point to the right, although most of the material may be in the left side of the container. A *left-handed arrangement* is, of course, exactly the opposite. The arranger should decide whether the composition should be right- or left-handed when he or she sees the plant materials, because the better side of the plant material must show and that may necessitate placement in a specific direction.

The *color combinations* in Japanese flower arrangements do not always please Occidentals. The Japanese combine strong warm colors, which are considered male, with pale, weak, and sometimes cool colors, which are considered female. Brilliant scarlet with pale orchid or light blue is often combined in Japanese kimonos and in flower arrangements. A pleasing custom, however, is to use light colors for H, M, and E and dark colors for any additional material used between them.

RIKKA OR RIKKWA

The first definite style or form developed by the earliest Japanese school of flower arrangement, the Ikenobo, was a complex foliage arrangement that was often about six feet tall. It was usually symmetrical or nearly so. In this arrangement several branches were made to appear as if they were growing from one central trunk. These different foliages were intended to suggest a bit of natural scenery: for example, pine might represent rocks and white flowers might symbolize a stream or a waterfall. Rikka arrangements were made in formal, stemmed bronze or large, tall bamboo containers.

These intricate arrangements took several days to compose, so only priests and the nobles had time to make them. The Ikenobo masters still create complex Rikka but they also make simplified variations for general use by their students. Arrangers of today should study pictures of Rikka compositions for inspiration.

Rikka arrangements may be formal, semi-formal, or informal. A *formal* arrangement has a tall, straight, central line. A *semi-formal* arrangement has a shorter central branch, often bent in dramatic lines, and wider side branches. An *informal* arrangement has two distinct divisions in its composition, and is used mostly at weddings.

The usual Rikka design is fairly symmetrical; it consists of a central branch and four side branches, the two on one side pointing downward at the end, the two on the other side pointing upward. Flowers of any color may be placed against the central branch.

All five placements may be of one kind of foliage, or some or all may be different. English yew, photinia, cedar, euonymus, oleander, or other compact spikes are the easiest to use. The pruning season should provide plenty of materials for Rikka arrangements. Sasanqua or other camellia foliage might well be used in this way when the plants are cut back for grafting.

American students seem to enjoy making modern adaptations of Rikka. This exercise teaches them to appreciate the beauty and variety in branches and foliage, and how to display them in organized compositions. Complete directions for making a Rikka adaptation are given on page 203.

SEIKA, CLASSICAL STYLE

The Seika style was created about 1450 A.D., because the ruler, Yoshimasa, wanted flower arrangements to be of a reasonable style and size so that the people could learn to arrange flowers and foliage for their homes.

Seika is a classical, dignified, formal style that permits only one method of design and has many restricting conventions. The general shape of a Seika is always triangular; its three separate parts or tips form a triangle when seen from the front and also when seen from above. The three required parts of the Seika are Heaven in the center, Man on one side, and Earth on the opposite side. These three basic lines usually have *helpers* which may be added between any of the lines, but never below them. The bare stems of all the plant materials are held tightly together like one stem or tree trunk for a number of inches above the rim of the container. No plant materials may touch the rim in a Seika arrangement.

The *proportions* used in a classical arrangement vary. Plants that naturally grow tall, such as cattails, are allowed to look tall in the arrangement, regardless of rules. Thirds are favorite proportions, halves are never used.

The width of an arrangement is important too. The most slender Seika arrangements are called formal, the wider arrangements semiformal, and the widest informal. Some of the informal Seikas have almost horizontal lines; they are the only classical arrangements that may be made in low containers.

The traditional containers for classical arrangements are of medium height or tall; the usubata, straight cylindrical vase, and bamboo are favorites. Other tall containers are also used for semi-formal Seika arrangements.

The *plant materials* that are available determine the kind of classical arrangement you can make. With pussy willow, Scotch broom, photinia, aspidistra, or any other flexible, non-branching spikes you can reproduce the beautiful curves of the classical arrangements. You can soak your materials and wire them into position overnight and they will retain their curves.

Other plant materials, such as woody branches, dock, snake grass, and long-stemmed flowers like stock, lupine, deliphinium, foxglove, lilies, or roses, are suitable for adaptations whether or not their stems can be curved.

Directions for making a classical adaptation are given on page 204.

NAGEIRE (Nag-e-ir-e)

The Nageire style of arrangement developed in the sixteenth century along with the tea ceremony and tea houses, because the tea masters felt they needed natural, informal flower arrangements. The term Nageire literally means "throw-in." Although Nageire arrangements are made to look casual, they are carefully designed. They are like the classical arrangements in that they have the three basic lines or levels, Heaven, Man, and Earth, but they may lean at any angle as in nature. The stems are close together.

Among the best *plant materials* to use for the Heaven and Man lines are foliage or fruit-tree branches or twigs, although the Earth line may consist of flowers. The entire arrangement may be made of flowers; a few that are suitable for Nageire are fuchsia, lupine, snapdragon, larkspur, tuberoses, carnations, and roses.

Nageire containers are always tall or medium in height. Containers may be made of any materials; wood, glass, pottery, or metal are effective and tall baskets and hanging containers are very popular. The containers have good form and no decoration. Some diagonal arrangements can be made without stem holders: the plants just lean against the container's edge and the stem ends are cut slanting so as to fit flat against the opposite side of the container. The traditional stem holders consist of one or two branched sticks placed across the inside of the container about two inches below the rim. For a cylindrical container two freshly cut sticks may be crossed and tied together firmly at the center. A heavy foliage branch may be split at the end and a cross piece inserted in the split, then tied in place to support the branch in the container.

Three kinds of Nageire are considered here: *standing* (upright, vertical), *lateral* (horizontal), and *hanging* (cascading, descending).

The *Standing Nageire* shows the Heaven, Man, and Earth placements in the same relative position as the classical. However, the stem ends are not stripped of leaves and are not held tightly together, and the tip of the Heaven line need not be over its base. The mouth of the vase may be partially covered with foliage or flowers. Plants which naturally stand straight are used for these arrangements.

The *Lateral Nageire* and the *Hanging Nageire* usually show the long Man line slanting sideways or downward, with the short Earth line above the container pointing in the opposite direction, and a medium length Heaven line between them usually pointing upward. Branches that naturally grow sideways and downward are used for these arrangements. They are sometimes called "over-the-cliff" arrangements. Lateral and Cascading arrangements are suggested by the trees growing horizontally from the mountain sides in Japan.

The *proportions* of Nageire arrangements vary; the primary branch may be one and one-half to three times the height of the container.

Nageire arrangements are the easiest of the Japanese arrangements for Westerners to make. They are useful in American homes, for they may be used with any kind of furnishings. Detailed directions for making a Nageire adaptation are given on page 206.

MORIBANA

The Moribana style developed at the end of the nineteenth century, when European houses and furnishings began to be used in Japan. Full, free-standing, informal flower arrangements were needed to go with Western furnishings and on Western dining tables so the Moribana (many flowers) style was created. The style is popular in Japan today, because the arrangements can be made quickly and easily and they vary greatly. The three most important kinds of Moribana arrangements are the *Flower Moribana,* the *Landscape Moribana,* and the *Morimono* (fruit, vegetable, and foliage).

One of the characteristics of all Moribana arrangements is that they are made in low containers, on pin-point stem holders, enabling the arranger to use short-stemmed flowers as well as tall ones.

A Moribana is *triangular in shape,* with Heaven, Man, and Earth at the three extreme points. Two additional groups are usually added, making five distinct parts all of different heights. Each one of these parts is also somewhat triangular in shape.

The different parts of the Moribana may be entirely separated from one another, each standing on its own pin-point holder. A favorite composition is to have Heaven and Man together and to have Earth at the extreme opposite diagonal position in the tray so that it completes the triangle and helps the balance.

Moribana arrangements are *balanced by placement.* They are higher at one side than the other so that they have imbalance unless they are placed off-side on a base, shelf, or table. Usually the heavier side of the arrangement is placed closer to its end of the base than the lighter side is to its end of the indicated space.

A Moribana arrangement may be lower in proportion to its width than other Japanese arrangements. An average dimension is to have the Heaven line one and one-half times the width of the container, with Man two-thirds of H and Earth one-third of H. Different schools use different proportions for Moribana. However, a fine branch of non-conforming proportions is used freely in any school without regard for conventional dimensions.

Either more or less than half of the water surface should be visible in a Moribana. The seasons, however, affect this proportion, and in the rainy season more water is shown.

Moribana expresses *the current season* by the choice of plant materials and the density of the arrangement too. In winter the plant materials are sparse, in spring and autumn they are of medium density, and in summer flowers are used profusely.

Plant materials used in Moribana arrangements should be placed in their natural relative positions: tree foliage is placed highest, foliage or flowers from shrubs come next, and ground flowers and grasses are at the bottom. Two kinds of tree foliage are not used together, but tree and shrub foliage may be combined. Moribana style is usually adopted for water plants because the low containers allow some water to show.

The Flower Moribana. Any appropriate kinds of flowers and foliage may be used in a Flower Moribana. One, two, three, five, or seven kinds of materials may be used together in one arrangement. Odd numbers of kinds are considered to be lucky. Stock, water-lilies, calla-lilies, camellias on stems, and roses are among the flowers used alone for Moribana. However, combinations of flowers and foliage are usually more interesting and more economical for gardeners. Heaven, Man, and Earth may consist of buds only, with open flowers for the helpers.

Divided root, a pleasing form of Flower Moribana, shows entirely separated groups of plant materials. Sometimes a water-hyacinth plant or a lotus bud with leaves is enough for the separate Earth group, regardless of the materials used in the larger groups. Iris looks well in three or five entirely separated groups of different heights, with the total effect a triangle.

The Flower Moribana may be made in either the forward part of the container or the rear. The proportions are not the same in the different positions. Full directions for making a Flower Moribana adaptation are given on page 207.

Other variations of Moribana are also possible, such as combinations of Nageire and Moribana. Some flower arrangements are especially suitable for table decoration; in them the stem holder is usually at one side of the container and Heaven and Man are nearly horizontal on opposite sides of the container, with a short Earth upright over the stem holder. Moribana is a flexible style and lends itself to personal taste and special use.

The Landscape Moribana. This is sometimes called a Nature Sketch or a Memory Sketch. It is a three-dimensional landscape that reproduces an outdoor scene in miniature. Branches with small leaves, such as live oak or box, are pruned to represent trees. Rocks or weathered wood may be used to suggest mountains. Very tiny flowers or small figurines of animals or human beings may be used in these pictures; everything must be in proper scale with the miniature trees.

A landscape usually expresses the current season in its plant materials and theme. In the winter bare branches and pine are suitable beside a narrow stream. In the summer a pond picture may show more water than anything else for its cooling effect. Chartreuse and yellow in the spring, and red and orange in the autumn also express the seasons.

The landscape composition is triangular and has three main groups or lines: Heaven, Man, and Earth. In the most simple landscapes the stem holder is usually placed in one of the rear corners of an oblong container. The longest branch, Heaven, may take a diagonal direction toward the opposite front corner, sometimes extending beyond the container. Man may be a short line in the opposite direction. Earth may be very insignificant, possibly just a rock. In this composition there is no vertical upright; however, these positions may be changed to suit plant materials.

In a divided (water-viewing or fish-path) composition Earth is usually a small, entirely separate group, often made up of its own H, M, and E. An empty water area separates the two main groups. Sometimes a landscape or waterscape is made up of five separate but closely related groups, all of different heights, and all within a triangular design.

Morimono. A Morimono arrangement consists essentially of fruits and vegetables. While it may also contain foliage, flowers are usually excluded.

Among suitable Morimono containers are a large leaf, bamboo

raft, weathered wood, metal tray, or pottery dish. A special pin-point holder in its own water container is used for foliage.

A Morimono composition follows closely the rules that guide the Moribana arrangement of flowers. A triangular arrangement is always desirable, with the largest materials hiding the stem holder at the base of the tallest line. A branch, a low plant, or a strong vine give the height needed in a fruit arrangement.

MODERN JAPANESE ARRANGEMENTS

Today, flower arrangement exhibitions in Tokyo show many entries that disregard traditional Japanese styles. Most of these free-form entries are ultra-modern, dramatic, imaginative and spectacular. Dry and fresh materials are combined well. Modern Japanese arrangers express their inherited restrained good taste in their contemporary arrangements.

Some of the most important schools of flower arrangement in Tokyo teach both the traditional and modern Japanese arrangements. Some schools stress their work with foreigners and provide English-speaking teachers.

PROBLEMS IN ADAPTATIONS OF JAPANESE FLOWER ARRANGEMENTS

(Suggestions from which to choose)

1. Make an adaptation of a Japanese classical arrangement using the three lines Heaven, Man, and Earth, in a container of medium height (see page 131). Gladiolus, stock, dock, yew, pussy willow, Scotch broom, or any tall spikes may be used. Do not have a focal area.
2. Make an "over-the-cliff" adaptation of a Nageire arrangement in a tall container (see page 132). Hold the stems tightly together.
3. Make an adaptation of a Landscape Moribana arrangement of the fish-path type (divided) in a low container (see page 132).
4. Make an adaptation of a Flower Moribana using five separate placements in a total triangle, in a low container.
5. Make an arrangement showing Japanese influence, using tree foliage for Heaven and Man and lower-growing foliage for Earth.

A NAGEIRE ADAPTATION, over-the-cliff type.

A MORIBANA ADAPTATION, a rock garden.

PART V

Types of Arrangements

Line
Line-Mass
Mass

Chapter 13

LINE ARRANGEMENTS

Flower and foliage arrangements of today may be generally classified as line, mass, or line-mass ("massed line") arrangements. A *line arrangement* emphasizes line; a *mass arrangement* emphasizes mass (and color); a *line-mass arrangement* combines both line and mass effects.

Line arrangements have developed greatly in the United States since our study of Japanese flower arrangement. The Japanese have been masters of line arrangements for centuries. This subject is presented in Chapter 12.

A line arrangement may be defined as one in which the lines are of foremost importance and the plant material is sparse. In a flower show an entry in a class entitled line arrangements must not have much plant material at the base or it will be classified as a line-mass arrangement.

Line arrangements often have special expressive qualities of theme and mood difficult to achieve in other arrangements. They convey a dynamic feeling of action and movement that cannot be obtained in mass arrangements. Line arrangements are symbolic of activity and life, and are vibrant, moving, slender, and youthful. Line arrangements encourage creative experimentation and originality because they feature the natural lines of the plant materials and do not conform to any set patterns.

The *chief characteristics* of good line arrangements are *restraint* and *clarity of line*. Limitation in the quantity of plant material used is essential; a good line arrangement shows that it is the product of thoughtful restraint. Simplicity is one of the qualities of superiority in flower arrangement, as it is in the other arts.

Clarity of line is essential in line arrangements. The leading lines must stand out, clean-cut and strong, so that they will be dominant in the design. These lines should be so compelling that an observer does not pause long at any particular place but continues to follow the lines with ease. The lines may be adorned with leaves or flowers but they should not be obscured. It is usually necessary to remove some leaves, twigs, or flowers from any material that is used.

Art Principles. *Rhythm* is the most important principle to consider in making a line arrangement. The subordinate lines should follow the leading line except possibly for some short opposing lines at the base. Any lines that disturb the rhythm should be pruned away, including crossing lines, straight horizontals, and monotonous, repetitious, or inconsequential lines.

Dominance of line over everything else including color and texture is to be expected in a line arrangement. Since the line element is featured, it seems unnecessary to have another center of interest or focal area. Americans, however, usually prefer to have a focal area in line arrangements to add color, variety, and weight. The leading line usually continues down into the focal area, which may be merely a broadening and reinforcing of the main line to give additional strength and stability at the base. The focal area should be subordinate to the line material if possible. Round flowers placed at the center of interest hold the attention too long, therefore oval or pointed flowers, or seed pods, are better, and they should point in the same direction as the leading line.

Balance in line arrangements is usually asymmetrical, for the scalene triangle (all sides unlike) is the most popular shape employed. Sometimes, however, modern stylized line arrangements are symmetrical, often with dramatic architectural effects. Since line arrangements are sparse they encourage experimentation in balance.

Proportion must be considered carefully, because it is easy to use a container too large for the sparse materials employed in a line arrangement. The test of proper proportion is to have more area in plant materials than in the container and base. Since the lines are usually slender they can extend several times the height or length of the containers without making arrangements seem top-heavy or too tall. Large line arrangements are effective as room decoration, but small ones merely decorate the surfaces on which they stand.

Radiation is important in line arrangements, since all the stems should meet at the same place on the small stem holder.

Variation is necessary in the silhouette of a line arrangement, and the voids must be carefully planned so they are different in size and shape. The solids, too, should vary in length and thickness and in power of attractiveness. Where so little material is presented, every item should be different from the others in some respect in order to prevent monotony.

Transition from density at the heart of the arrangement to thinness at the extremities is achieved by adding plant material at the base, and also by removing any large leaves or flowers toward the outer ends of the lines.

Plant Materials for Line Arrangements. Some plant materials are suitable for line arrangements and some are not; for example, spirea sprays are usable but peonies are not. A few branches from a flowering pear, plum, or cherry tree could form an excellent line arrangement, but would be wasted in a mass effect.

Some other good line materials are fuchsia, barberry, variegated privet, Scotch broom, and dogwood. You can also make line arrangements entirely of foliage or of buds which have beauty of form and in addition contain the promise of later beauty. You can bend some straight branches or stems into desired curves. Weathered dry twigs or roots are practical for permanent line arrangements to which a few living flowers may occasionally be added.

Homemakers will find that line arrangements are economical, since they can be made with small amounts of plant materials. Even women who have no gardens can sometimes find interesting weeds and other suitable line materials along roads and in vacant lots.

PROBLEMS IN LINE ARRANGEMENTS
(Suggestions from which to choose)

1. Make a line arrangement of five strong stems of ivy radiating from one point in a bowl.
2. Make a line arrangement with diagonal or horizontal lines, in a low container (see page 159).
3. Make a downward-pointing line arrangement in a tall green or brown bottle using vines such as ivy, wisteria, or philodendron.
4. Make an arrangement using a weathered stick or branch for the main line.
5. Judge the arrangements made in class. Eliminate the less worthy half and point score the others (see page 234).

FEMININE QUALITY IN GRACEFUL S CURVE. The three textures have affinity, the pewter container agreeing with the zinnias and corn tassels. The third dimension (depth) is well shown here, for the uppermost zinnias face to the rear and the lowest lines of corn extend forward. Scotch broom or pussy willow might also have been used in place of the corn.

144

NATURAL LINE-MASS ARRANGEMENT of two well-chosen branches of white crape-myrtle. The most compact mass makes a focal area near the rim of the container. Keeping one end of the container empty gives style. The vertical axis goes through the center of the container, with equal weight on each side of it; therefore the arrangement is self balanced and may stand in the center of a mantel shelf. The container is a narrow, heavy pottery piece by Russel Wright.

145

Chapter 15

MASS ARRANGEMENTS

A mass arrangement may be defined as one that emphasizes a large mass of flowers as a whole unit, rather than individual branches or flowers. A mass arrangement always has a thick, full-bodied look. Since mass arrangements require a large quantity of flowers and also suggest seasonal abundance, gardeners usually make them in summer and autumn when their flowers are most plentiful.

Many trained flower arrangers dislike mass arrangements because they do not allow the plant materials to show at their best. The general public, however, likes them and florists sell many of them. They are especially suitable when done in scale for large rooms. Occasions of importance can usually be well expressed by large, impressive, formal mass arrangements. They are generally used for cemetery arrangements. Some themes in flower shows suggest lavish displays of masses of flowers. Two different kinds of mass arrangements, *period type arrangements* and *stylized arrangements*, are usually exhibited in American flower shows. *Natural mass arrangements* are used mostly in homes.

Period Type Arrangements (see Chapter 11). Most period arrangements are mass arrangements. True copies of period styles are sometimes exhibited in flower shows for educational purposes; however, the schedules usually call for an *adaptation* of a specific period, an arrangement *influenced by* a specific period, or one *in the manner* of a specific period. A flower arranger of today tries to express the *mood* of the historic period rather than its accurate details.

For home use an arranger has much leeway in making traditional

146

mass arrangements. Flowers from the garden may be used and the design freely adapted to suit the furnishings.

Early American furnishings call for plain, primitive containers and sturdy plant materials, simply arranged, without stylization.

Colonial adaptations are usually large, exuberant, colorful, elegant, and asymmetrical, and are made in reproductions of traditional containers.

Federal (post-Revolutionary) adaptations are tall, slender, symmetrical, pale, fine textured, and well designed, and made in classical containers.

Empire (Napoleonic) adaptations are large, richly colored, strongly textured, and masculine, and are often placed in containers suggesting Egyptian or Roman forms.

Victorian adaptations are large, broad, curvaceous, asymmetrical, fine textured, cool colored, and spotty, often made in decorated containers.

Mixed combinations of old furniture, found in many homes, call for rather old-fashioned mass arrangements. These bouquets usually have no particular characteristics except that they are full-fashioned and may include any garden flowers.

Stylized Mass Arrangements. These arrangements are smart, up-to-date, and truly American, for they express young America's desire for clean-cut designs. Stylized arrangements should be firmly based on the principles of good design. Three or more kinds of flowers are usually combined; the plant materials are segregated, therefore each variety is plainly seen. Colors are segregated, too, and placed in patterns having rhythm. The center of interest is well designed and located at the core of the arrangement. The silhouette is carefully planned.

Stylized mass arrangements can not be made without generous quantities of the *same materials*. For example, a large, free-standing stylized arrangement for a formal tea table in a large room requires about four dozen spikes of one kind, three dozen shorter spikes or secondary materials, and three dozen target flowers, as roses, for the center of interest. Small quantities of many kinds of flowers can not be made into a stylized arrangement. Flowers with strong stems that can be controlled and placed in definite spots are necessary for such precise designs.

The forms or shapes of stylized mass arrangements vary greatly. Pyramids with more or less open sides are appropriate for formal teas. Low symmetrical domes are standard designs for dining-table centerpieces. Right-angled triangles, crescents, semi-circles, or S curves become stylized mass arrangements by the addition of sufficient volume at the central part of the design.

Stylized mass arrangements may be used in homes with modern or traditional furnishings, depending upon the kind of plant materials that are employed. They do not suit primitive, natural, or unstudied backgrounds. They may be used for church or platform decoration as well as for formal table decoration for important occasions.

Natural Mass Arrangements. Sometimes a compact flowering branch or spray of flowers makes a very satisfactory natural mass arrangement. For example, a thickly-flowered branch of azaleas or some fully-branching stems of crotalaria or cosmos can form large, pleasing, natural mass arrangements.

Foliage, too, makes attractive mass arrangements. Pittosporum or pine is particularly effective used alone or with other leaves for floor arrangements. Natural mass arrangements of colorful leaves are expressive of the woods in autumn; driftwood makes a happy addition to such an arrangement.

Art Principles. The art principles apply to all mass arrangements. *Proportion* suggests that a mass arrangement should not have similar dimensions in its height and breadth, and that the total area of the plant materials must be at least one and one-half times as large as the area of the container and base. *Balance* calls for a strong vertical stalk and a compact effect at the center of a mass arrangement. *Rhythm* in mass arrangements is achieved largely through color placed in linear patterns. *Dominance* of one kind of plant material and one color is important in a composite arrangement. Emphasis on a center of interest is necessary where so much variety occurs. *Variation* is desirable in mass arrangements. Several varieties of plant materials are usually combined to produce a good design.

Airiness is a goal to be sought even in mass arrangements. Open space should be left for the flowers to "breathe" and to move in the breeze.

The *third dimension* is important in mass arrangements. Lines that extend forward over the rim of the container are usually desirable. Lines and areas should be designed for depth to lead the eye back through the plant materials.

PROBLEMS IN MASS ARRANGEMENTS
(Suggestions from which to choose)

1. Draw an outline of a bisymmetrical mass arrangement with large, high side voids in an urn-shaped container without handles.
2. Draw an outline of an asymmetrical mass arrangement in a large low circular container on a base.
3. Make an airy free mass arrangement using three kinds of plant materials, one of which is wild roadside material.
4. Make a long, low, bisymmetrical free-standing mass arrangement for the dining table, using flower spikes like larkspur, snapdragon, lupine, or gladiolus for the extending material and roundish flowers for the central focal area.
5. Make an upright, front-faced oval mass arrangement from a mixture of cool-colored garden flowers against a background of gray foliage. Have the longest stems on the smallest flowers, medium stems on the medium-size flowers, and shortest stems on the biggests flowers. Let the lines radiate from one place.
6. Make a mass arrangement of foliage using green, yellow-green, or blue-green in different values.

ROCOCO INFLUENCE. Many general characteristics of Rococo style are used here: asymmetrical balance, small size, feminine quality, Oriental influence, lack of scale, and many curves. The pink and white Japanese quince and camellias in a white alabaster container give a gay and glamorous effect.

PART VI

Some Appropriate Arrangements

For the Home
Church, Club, and Christmas Decorations
Non-Floral Arrangements

Chapter 16

FLOWER ARRANGEMENTS
FOR THE HOME

Most flower arrangers are primarily interested in the decoration of their homes. Flowers provide an important *living quality* as well as the beauty of color and fine texture that are needed as relief from the hard metals, woods, plastics, and fabrics that comprise the interiors of our homes. Flower arrangements smile their welcome in the entrance hall; they enhance and accent the beauty of the living room; and they add cheer to the dining room. They express the care and the love that make a home; they enrich the life of a family. Flower arrangements in a home help to develop aesthetic interests in all its members.

Home gardeners should grow some cutting flowers to suit the interiors of their houses in color, texture, and mood. A modern house needs large, bold, colorful flowers, while a traditional house suggests the more conventional flowers. A variety of interesting foliage plants should also be grown for use in arrangements.

Living-Room Arrangements. A living room can usually accommodate three flower or foliage arrangements of different sizes. They may stand on the piano, mantel shelf, occasional table, coffee table, book shelf, television or radio cabinet, or on the floor. Usually one large arrangement is dominant; this featured one might well be placed close to the center of interest. All the arrangements should have some relation to one another in *mood, style,* and *color.*

154

A *piano arrangement* should preferably be a dry arrangement so that there is no danger of spilled water. For a grand piano an arrangement should usually be large, low, heavy, and curved to harmonize with the form of the instrument. The beautiful finish of a piano precludes the use of coarse materials on it.

A *mantel arrangement* must not be too large or too thick or it will appear unstable. In a formal, symmetrical room the mantel arrangement may be symmetrical, too, and may stand in the middle of the mantel shelf; or two identical but reversed asymmetrical arrangements may balance one another on the ends of the shelf and possibly point toward some accessory in the center. One asymmetrical arrangement on a symmetrical mantel should not stand far from center unless it is well balanced by some object. When the fireplace and mantel are asymmetrical, the flower arrangement should also be asymmetrical. An arrangement should not cover any part of a picture, but it usually looks well before a mirror. Downward-hanging things are possible on the mantel, but they seldom look trim and architectural.

The American-born artist James McNeill Whistler used to spend hours arranging beautiful things on his mantel shelf. It behooves a homemaker to spend plenty of time finding exactly the right containers and accessories to use on the mantel shelf for they express and reveal her personality and taste.

A *table arrangement* for the living room must agree in scale with the table on which it stands. An occasional table (usually portable) should have a fairly low and steady arrangement.

A *coffee-table arrangement* should be presentable from all sides and also from above. Usually these arrangements are fairly small, low, and compact so that they will not upset easily or crowd the serving tray. The style of the table must be considered; for example, succulents look well on a modern coffee table. Fragrant flowers are usually favorites. Small flowers like pansies or violets combine well with a decorative rock for a coffee table arrangement.

A *book-shelf arrangement* gives pleasing variety in a cleared area on one of the higher shelves. It is usually fairly low and long. A manzanita, sage, or trimmed pine branch extending to one side is appropriate, with cones at the focal area occasionally replaced by fresh flowers.

A *television or radio-cabinet arrangement* is usually of secondary importance in a living room and is seldom large. Music cabinets suggest rhythm, and this is best expressed by line or line-mass effects. An arrangement should harmonize with the size, shape, and color of any picture above the cabinet; if there is no picture a vertical arrangement is suitable. A dry arrangement is safe and satisfactory for a music cabinet.

Dining-Room Arrangements (see page 8). The color scheme and style of the dining room affect the arrangements used in it. One or two arrangements are sufficient in the average room.

A *buffet or sideboard arrangement* may be featured if the dining-table arrangement is fairly small. The arrangement on the buffet should be one-faced and may be as large as desired. A wine cooler, tall cake dish, compote, or soup tureen would make a good container. No important accessories should be placed on the buffet to compete with the arrangement. For every-day use a long-lasting mixed foliage arrangement is excellent on the buffet.

A *dinner-table arrangement* for the average home as a rule is low enough not to interfere with the diners' view of one another. The basic design for a centerpiece for a dinner table for six or more is a fairly low one with upstanding material in the center and horizontal extensions at the ends; however, the ultimate design depends on the available plant materials. A centerpiece may be made in a container of glass, porcelain, pottery, or metal, whichever is most harmonious with the table equipment being used.

A *breakfast arrangement* should be something cheerful to lift the spirits of the family and send them out with chins up. A casual airy effect is better than anything studied or complicated. A breakfast table may be small, so the arrangement is usually rather small and free-standing, made of modest flowers in unpretentious containers.

Bedroom Arrangements. The dresser, chest, desk, or table in a bedroom may hold a flower arrangement. It should express the personality of the occupant. Restful effects are usually appropriate.

A *bedside-table arrangement* should be quite small and so low that it is not easily upset. The flowers should be in prime condition. Fragrant flowers are especially pleasing. For a sick person a flower known to be a favorite is desirable; an orchid, however, is perfect since it need not be placed in water. A bedside tray with food wants only a miniature or a single flower as adornment.

A *dressing-table arrangement* in a woman's room might include a real fan as a background for flowers. If the dressing-table space is limited a slender vertical arrangement would, however, be more practical.

A *high-chest arrangement* in a man's room should not be a temporary one. A dry arrangement in browns would be fitting, possibly of ceiling height. Drama could be given by rough textures. A man's hobby can sometimes be featured in a composition for his room.

A *landscape composition* in a frame would be desirable for a boy's room. Some carved wooden animals, a driftwood tree, rocks, and sand would be enough for a three-dimensional landscape.

Hall Arrangements. The most feasible place for an arrangement in the hall is on a table underneath a mirror. Such a location usually calls for height and light colors. The style and mood of the hall arrangement should be a keynote for designs throughout the house.

Patio or Terrace Arrangements. Flower and foliage arrangements for patios, porches, or terraces should usually be rather casual and natural in effect, not severely stylized in design. Outdoor table arrangements should be low and solid so that wind will not upset them. The containers and the plant materials are generally strongly textured for outdoor use. Sturdy flowers, foliage, vegetables, fruits, or berries are suitable in containers of metal, pottery, wood, or driftwood. Large jars of foliage are effective in outdoor settings.

PROBLEMS IN ARRANGEMENTS FOR THE HOME
(Suggestions from which to choose)

1. Make a coffee table arrangement in a plain dark saucer or similar container, placing a pyramid-like rock off-center and using succulents or pansies or other materials with it.

IN THE LIVING ROOM. A horizontal arrangement is correct in shape for the top of a piano beneath a picture. The subject is a pink house and a pinkish garden in Villefranche on the Mediterranean. The flowers repeat the colors in the painting and suggest the fragrances in this land of the perfume makers. The picture was painted by the author of this book.

CH
Wi
tair
the
sch
cov
the
desi
S
targ
Wi
thir
peel
cont
side
strik
way
sam
B
One
mor
tabl
mee
priv
men
cent
Y
blue,
valu
need
may
flowe
wate
the d
A
banq
pitto

Chapter 17

CHURCH, CLUB, AND
CHRISTMAS DECORATIONS

CHURCH ARRANGEMENTS

Church arrangements should be attractive enough to interest the congregation but not so spectacular as to compete with the minister for attention. They must of course conform to any regulations concerning the specific church to be decorated.

Expressiveness is considered to be important in church arrangements. Although all plant material is expressive of the Creator, a beautiful arrangement also expresses the love, care, and talent of one of His people. To express the dignity and formality desirable in churches, large arrangements may be made of tall stately flowers in symmetrical designs. Aspiration and hope are also best expressed by tall arrangements reaching heavenward. The mood of a small church with simple interior architecture would be well expressed by any wild flowers or garden flowers or foliages that are suitable.

The *design* of a church arrangement is not standardized, but may be of any type, style, or size that suits the specific spot where it is to stand. Line, line-mass, or mass arrangements that are natural, semi-stylized, or stylized are all acceptable, depending on the background. Since a church interior is high, it is often advisable to use vertical floral decorations. Large arrangements are, of course, consistent with the scale of most churches. Usually the arrangement is

161

need not be in water. In it at intervals may be inserted similar low small arrangements of flowers in containers. This is a precise, compact effect much superior to the stringy trailing ivy sometimes used.

CHRISTMAS DECORATIONS

Christmas is a time of extra festivity and joy and it is expressed in the decorations of the season. Glitter and tinsel and brightness are not confined to the Christmas tree. Foliage, fruit, seed vessels, grain, and branches may be sprayed or painted snowy white, gilt, silver, or copper for use during this season. These natural materials are of course considered to be much superior to the artificial imitations now procurable. The painted natural materials are usually arranged in containers like other dry arrangements, with full attention to all the principles of design. Bright Christmas balls of one color but different sizes may be added to an arrangement of painted materials for additional sparkle.

The silvered materials look well on the dining table with its silver flatware. Some fresh flowers may be added to the silvered table arrangement. The white arrangements are needed in the hall or wherever there is scant light. The gilded materials usually add interest to a mantel shelf, especially if they are near a gilded mirror frame and brass hardware. The gilded and coppered materials look well together. All the arrangements in one room should have some relation in their plant materials and in color. Two or three arrangements are usually enough for one room.

The Christmas wreath or swag outside on the front door is usually made of long-lasting natural greens and something colorful tied with plastic weatherproof ribbon. The greens are consistent with the outdoor surroundings. A Della Robbia type wreath of unpainted nuts, seed vessels, fruit, and foliage is a welcome change from the gilded and silvered materials and is more suitable for some homes. Only unpainted materials should be used in the same room with this natural wreath.

It is not desirable to upset the decorative scheme of a home by hanging greens and other materials here and there, over pictures, on stairways, or in corners, except of course for the indispensable mistletoe hanging high somewhere.

The Christmas tree is usually made gay and bright with many colors. However it is possible to obtain a cool, solemn, holy-night effect by using only blue lights on the tree, indoors or outdoors, thus giving a touch of distinction and unusual beauty.

PROBLEMS
(Suggestions from which to choose)

1. Make a tall, formal, bisymmetrical church arrangement in a tall container (see page 16).
2. Make a tea party centerpiece suitable for some festive occasion. Use a container with a tall stem if possible; hang some material over the edges.
3. Make a foliage arrangement suitable for the floor of a lecture platform (see page 169).
4. Paint some pine, camellia, and magnolia leaves silver for your Christmas table centerpiece. Use white or pink flowers or Christmas balls with it (see page 169).
5. Make a gilded arrangement of several materials in a turquoise-colored container. Add some turquoise balls for the focal area.
6. Make a door wreath or swag. Start with a wire clothes hanger. Pull it into a round shape, leave the hook on it. Wrap the hanger thickly with cedar twigs, using fine wire to secure them. Wire your ornaments to the cedar wreath. Tie a waterproof bow at the top.
7. Make a large, low, coffee table arrangement of gilded pine or magnolia leaves, with coppered pine cones and clusters of coppered, wired acorns.

A TABLE DECORATION. Whoever has a variegated pittosporum bush need never be without living decoration for an unexpected event. The candles set in greenish pottery holders frame the dinner table centerpiece between them.

PINK FOR THE TEA TABLE. With green and pink caladium leaves, a complementary color scheme is devised with rosa de montaña and hibiscus in pink, crinum in pink and white, and a green glass container.

FOR PLATFORM OR FLOOR.
Wild cane plumes are used with
violet-red celosia to make a large
sleek stylized platform or floor arrangement. The design is chiefly
vertical but is modified by the curving lines of the celosia. Distinction
in texture is furnished by the velvety
celosia. These materials are dry
and they will endure for a long
time.

CHRISTMAS GILT. Dry monochromatic arrangements should
have dark and light contrasts. Here
the gilded sea-oats and dry cycad
leaves provide light-colored areas.
The brown container has gold flecks
in it, and the pine cones are gilded.
The dock spikes and magnolia leaves
are brown. It is a lively decoration
for a hall table especially at Christmas time.

as flower arrangements. If branches are used to form the skeleton
of the line or line-mass arrangements they can usually be bent into
curves to suit the design. Large branches of *Magnolia grandiflora*
may be arranged in S curves in tall floor jars; they are handsome
enough to use at church weddings. Spikes of aspidistra leaves combined with a focal area of light green young paper-plant leaves look
well in a vertical design. A coffee table arrangement can be made
quickly from a whorl of loquat leaves radiating from one side of a
cushion of variegated pittosporum. Masses of colorful autumn leaves
should have several large voids even when they are arranged naturally with the emphasis on color. All foliage arrangements should
have some light and some dark values to bring out the designs.

Potted House Plants.   Large foliage plants in pots are often important decorative notes, especially in modern houses where areas
are designed for them. Small foliage plants in pots are usually inef-
fective except in plant rooms where they are shown in numbers.
Various potted plants with leaves of different sizes and shapes may
be combined to make one unified composition.

FRUIT ARRANGEMENTS

Any homemaker would enjoy knowing how to make a presentable
fruit arrangement for those times when she has no flowers. Fruit
arrangements can be as lively and colorful as flower arrangements.
These arrangements are thrifty too, since their contents can be
eaten later. Most fruit arrangements in flower shows are overcrowded
and have too much variety. Restraint suggests that part of the container be left empty to rest the eyes.

All the design principles apply to fruit compositions. Transition in
size is very desirable. To obtain it a large object like a grapefruit
should be located at the focal point, with the middle sized fruit
adjoining that, and the small items like kumquats or grapes farthest
away. All stem ends should usually turn in the same direction for
rhythm. In a foliage arrangement, fruit may be impaled on sticks
and used for focal material; grapes may hang gracefully over the
rim. A simple beautiful low fruit composition can be made from

NON-FL

dry bleacl
in place
or leaves ¹
backgrour
of dock s|
to which

An im|
tered desi
values; da
color varia

The m(
stuck in a
holders or
the stems
impaled o
several hoı
the stems

WEATHI

Driftwoc
It is a fav(
tables. It i
delicate fl(
range of te
cleaned, bl(

Weather
form. Vari;
Different s
serve well a

Flower aı
compositioı
essary cont
is economic
a few leave
weathered ı

sections of grape vines with leaves and bunches of dark and light grapes and a few peaches placed on a bamboo raft. A hand of bananas provides variation in form and rhythm in a composition that has too many round forms.

The best color effects are definitely restrained. Purple, green, and white combinations are effective. Orange, yellow, and green make a pleasing analogy when placed in that order. Confusion results when such a variety as red, purple, and yellow occurs in one fruit composition. Leaves and flowers, with stems in concealed tubes of water or in small containers, can be used effectively with fruit or vegetables. Leaves may add the necessary height that is often lacking in these compositions.

Paintings of fruit by artists like Cézanne should be studied for design and color.

VEGETABLE ARRANGEMENTS

A vegetable composition must not appear like an assemblage on a sales counter. Usually part of the container should be empty for contrast and relief. An arranger might begin by placing one large object like an eggplant, melon, or artichoke on a large pin-point stem holder located at one side in a low container. This large object is the focal point and the smaller vegetables should usually be placed in areas and lines that lead toward it. As with fruit, stem ends should all turn in the same direction for rhythm.

Restrained color schemes are particularly desirable in vegetable compositions too, for the materials are often colorful. Loquat leaves, eggplants, turnips, and small white onions make a sparkling cool scheme. A warm harmony can be assembled with sansevieria leaves, a chartreuse melon, yellow squashes, and small yellow tomatoes. Striking materials like pink rhubarb stalks bearing their own chartreuse leaves are sometimes available and should receive special rewards in flower shows. Leaves or succulent plants often provide pleasing contrasts in vegetable compositions.

of driftwood may well be the center of attention in a composition.

Interesting driftwood is now often exhibited by itself. A large piece may be placed in the fireplace hole in summer, or hung on the wall like a bas-relief, or used for a garden feature. Driftwood that resembles living creatures is often used by children in their compositions. Collecting weathered wood is an experience in aesthetics because of the necessity for judging line and form.

WEED AND GRASS ARRANGEMENTS

Weed and grass arrangements may be fresh or dry materials or combinations of both. Those bearing seeds or seed pods are especially effective. Children should be taught to recognize the beauty in roadside materials, which are so readily available. Some of the best-looking weeds are dock, teasel, and milkweed, but many others are also attractive. Johnson grass seed plumes are airy and pretty; wild oats and other grasses make excellent spike materials.

Weed and grass arrangements should not suggest a bunch of sticks; their interesting forms should be allowed to show. One outstanding kind of weed or grass should dominate, while the others should merely accompany the main theme. Variety in the size and shape of those combined is desirable. These arrangements should look natural and unlabored even when they are designed with care. Containers for them should usually be rather casual, primitive, coarse, or rugged. Bottles and other tall containers are suitable in shape as the arrangements are usually tall.

LANDSCAPE COMPOSITIONS

Landscape compositions may be shallow bas-reliefs in frames to hang on walls or they may be deep, free-standing arrangements on plates or in niches. They may be made from dry or living materials or combinations of both.

Everything in a landscape composition must be in scale. In an ordinary non-landscape composition with figurines, true scale relations are not required: for example, the flower's face may be larger than the figurine's face. In a landscape composition, a branch that resembles a tree usually sets the scale, and the other things must be the right size for it. A dry tree-like branch may be used in a sandy desert scene with rocks representing mountains and suitable materials such as sage and donkeys in the foreground. A fresh sprig of live oak or boxwood with its small leaves may be the keynote for a brookside scene, with clumps of green grass and flowers in scale, and possibly ducks, turtles, or boys. There should be plenty of empty uncluttered space in a landscape composition; simplicity is an admirable quality there.

PROBLEMS IN NON-FLORAL ARRANGEMENTS
(Suggestions from which to choose)

1. Make a foliage arrangement of three kinds of leaves.
2. Make a vegetable arrangement in purple, white, and green, on a raft.
3. Make a dry line-mass arrangement with a cluster of pine cones, milk-weed pods, or lotus pods at the focal area.
4. Make a dry arrangement including several bunches of wheat or other grain in a horizontal, diagonal effect, on a mat (see page 38).
5. Make a driftwood or weathered wood composition.
6. Make a three-dimensional landscape on a plate or tray. Use a figurine and live oak or boxwood for a tree. Everything must be in consistent scale (see page 187).
7. Make a fruit and foliage arrangement in yellow, orange, and green, in a basket.
8. Make an arrangement of roadside materials such as weeds, grasses, and rocks (see page 187).
9. Point score five competitive coffee table arrangements made of foliage only. Award blue, red, and yellow ribbons as when judging in a flower show (see Chapter 25).

EMPHASIS ON MOOD. A painting of a church in Cordova, New Mexico, expresses a mood that is repeated in the dry composition below it. The weathered wood was placed so that it would extend over the edge of the picture frame to unite the two designs. Dry artichokes suggest the wild thistles of the region. This picture is an oil painting by Dr. Norman E. Rutt.

PART VII

The Making of Flower Arrangements

Preparation of Plant Materials
Containers
Mechanics of Flower Arranging
Directions for Making Flower Arrangements

Chapter 19

PREPARATION OF PLANT MATERIALS

Plant materials may be cut in the early morning, but preferably after sunset so that they can be placed in the dark after cutting. Cut with a sharp knife on a slant so that the ends will not rest flat on the bottom of the container. Put the stem ends immediately in water that has been carried into the garden. When you have brought the flowers indoors, remove the leaves from the lowest third or more of the stems so as not to foul the water. If you are sure that you do not want the leaves in the arrangement, remove nearly all of them. At the same time remove the thorns from the rose stems, using sandpaper for that purpose. Place the flowers in deep water up to their blossom heads in a cool, dark, draftless place for a few hours or overnight to condition them for arranging. Spray the plant materials with a cold water mist occasionally to counteract dehydration. Some arrangers reach down in the water and there cut an inch off the ends of stems so that air bubbles can not enter the stems. On the ends of stems that exude sap, rub salt or ashes.

Most flowers last longer if they are cut when in the bud stage or partly open. It is a pleasant experience to see them opening indoors. The shorter the stems, the longer the flowers usually last.

The keeping quality of cut flowers is increased if the water is changed daily. A bulb syringe may be used for that purpose. The whole arrangement may be set in deep water overnight. It should also be kept cool and away from draughts. Cut flowers may be kept in a refrigerator if the temperature can be maintained slightly warmer than is customary for food.

182

Certain chemicals help flowers to keep fresh by stopping their development. A very little Clorox, alum, or sugar may be added to the arrangement water for this purpose. Commercial preparations are available that are effective in making flowers last longer.

Woody branches are usually split, scraped, and crushed at the ends. They may also be dipped in salt solution and then burned.

Leaves may be dipped in a salt solution or salt may be rubbed on the stem ends just before arranging. Many leaves, such as those of canna, violet, caladium, hydrangea, and banana, should be submerged in cold water for a few hours or over night in order that they remain crisp in arrangements.

Burning the ends of stems over a flame is the best treatment for some flowers. Holding the stem ends in *boiling water* is preferable for other plants, especially water plants. Both these methods keep the pores in the stems open so that water can rise to the blossoms. Small stems require shorter boiling time than large ones. When burning or boiling the ends of stems the flowers must be protected by wrapping them in damp newspapers or a damp cloth and holding them as horizontal as possible. After either of these treatments the flowers or leaves are placed in deep, cold water for several hours before they are used in arrangements.

Many flowers and leaves do not need special treatment before they are arranged except the preliminary soaking in deep water. However, some materials last longer if they are given the treatments suggested here, and other materials require special treatment or they will not hold up long enough to be placed in arrangements.

Most recommendations for treating plant material in the following list were given to the author by her Japanese teachers of flower arrangement. In this list the solutions mentioned have these proportions: the peppermint solution is one-fourth teaspoon of the oil or essence to a quart of water, the hydrochloric acid solution is a 10% solution, the ordinary alcohol solution is one teaspoon to a quart of water, the strong alcohol solution is 20% alcohol.

The term "soak" here means to put the stems in deep water up to the neck of the flowers for 2 hours or more. "Submerge" means to cover entirely with water.

ACACIA: 5 minutes, stem ends in strong alcohol solution. Then soak.

AMARYLLIS: ½ hour in peppermint solution. Soak.

APPLE BLOSSOMS: 3 minutes in hydrochloric acid, alcohol, or peppermint solution. Soak.

ASTERS: 2 hours in sugar solution.

AZALEAS: Burning, or hydrochloric acid solution, or strong alcohol solution. Soak.

BAMBOO: 2 minutes in boiling vinegar. Submerge in cold water 1 hour. Soak.

BEGONIAS: 1 or 2 minutes in strong alcohol solution.

BROOM: Submerge several hours. Then shape and tie firmly.

CALLA-LILIES: 2 minutes in strong alcohol solution. Pinch of tobacco in arrangement water.

CAMELLIAS: 1 hour in slightly salty water. Put salt in the water after arranging. Do not touch flower heads.

CANNAS: ½ hour in hydrochloric acid solution.

CARNATIONS: Rub dry salt in ends of stems. 3 minutes in boiling water. Soak in water, not too cold.

CHERRY BLOSSOMS: 4 minutes in boiling water. Soak.

CHRYSANTHEMUMS: 4 minutes in boiling water. Then hold upside down and shower carefully with cold water, keeping inside of flower dry. Soak.

CLEMATIS: Cut some solid wood stem with it. Soak.

COLUMBINES: 2 minutes in peppermint or hydrochloric acid solution, or rub dry salt on stem ends. Soak.

COSMOS: 2 minutes in peppermint solution. Soak.

DAFFODILS: Place in very shallow water or they become water-soaked.

DAHLIAS: Growers' method is to place the stems in hot water and let it cool naturally. Then soak. Or soak in weak alcohol solution 2 hours.

DAISY (Shasta): Burn ends. Soak.

DAISY (Transvaal): 3 minutes in peppermint solution. Soak.

DOGWOOD: (If necessary) 4 minutes in hydrochloric acid or strong alcohol solution. Split end of stem. Soak.

FORGET-ME-NOTS: Boiling water, or 1 hour in weak alcohol solution.

FREESIAS: 2 or 3 hours in weak alcohol solution.

GARDENIAS: Spray with water, and keep in air-tight cellophane bag in refrigerator until used. Handle with wet hands only.

GLADIOLUS: 2 hours in weak alcohol or peppermint solution.

HELIOTROPE: 1 minute, burn or boil. Soak.

HOLLYHOCK: 3 minutes in peppermint solution. Soak.

HYACINTHS: 1 minute, boiling water or strong alcohol solution. Soak. Or 2 hours in weak alcohol solution.

HYDRANGEA: Crush stems, boil 5 minutes in vinegar. Soak. If possible cut some woody stem with the flower.

IRIS: 3 minutes in boiling water or 10 minutes in hot ashes. Wash off and soak. Cut in bud stage.

LARKSPUR: 1 hour in weak alcohol solution.

LILIES (Easter, tiger, and others): Burn stem ends. Remove stamens to keep flowers clean. Turn upside down under cold shower. Soak. Put sugar in arrangement water.

LILIES-OF-THE-VALLEY: 2 minutes in boiling water. Soak.

LOTUS BLOSSOMS: Cut leaf and flower stems while under water, inject alcohol in the stem. Soak. Or seal the ends with sealing wax immediately after cutting. Soak.

MAPLE LEAVES (autumn): 3 minutes in boiling vinegar. Soak.

MARGUERITES: 2 minutes in peppermint solution. Soak.

MARIGOLDS: 4 minutes in peppermint solution. Soak. Add 1 tablespoon sugar to arrangement water to remove odor.

MORNING GLORIES: Cut in bud stage. Burn. Soak.

NASTURTIUMS: 1 minute in boiling water. Soak.

PEACH BLOSSOMS: 4 minutes in boiling water. Soak.

PEONIES: Cut in bud stage. 5 minutes in boiling water. Then hold upside down in cold shower but keep inside of flower dry. Soak.

PINE: 10 minutes with stems in undiluted alcohol. Soak. Or merely soak.

PLUM BLOSSOMS: 5 minutes in boiling water. Soak.

POINSETTIAS: 3 minutes in boiling water, or 5 minutes in hydrochloric acid solution, or burn ends. Soak. Remove the leaves from the stem several days before cutting the flower off the plant.

POPPIES: Cut in the bud stage. Salt the stem ends, put in boiling water. Soak.

ROSES: Cut in bud stage. 2 minutes in boiling water or hydrochloric acid solution. Or burn stem ends. Soak in slightly salty water. Roll in damp newspaper to support stems. Keep cool.

SALVIA: 3 minutes in peppermint solution. Soak.

SWEET PEAS: 3 minutes in alcohol or 1 hour in weak alcohol solution.

TULIPS: 1 minute in boiling water, or 2 minutes in strong alcohol, or soak 2 hours in weak alcohol solution.

WATER-LILIES: Cut in morning. Inject alcohol in end of stem, or put a few drops of melted paraffin inside the flowers to keep them open at night. Soak.

WISTERIA: Cut after sunset. Burn stem ends, or put them in strong alcohol solution for five minutes. Soak.

JUNIOR ARRANGEMENTS

Top: Dry roadside materials and driftwood on a wood slab.

Bottom: Boxwood, rocks, and ceramic ducks on a plate of sand.

Top: Castor bean stalks in a large bronze container.

Bottom: A boxwood "tree" shelters the wooden Grandparents.

187

Chapter 20

CONTAINERS

The beauty of a flower arrangement depends in no small part on the container. It must agree with the plant materials in line, form, texture, color, and expressiveness. Therefore it is necessary for an efficient flower arranger to have a variety of containers from which to choose. At least twenty-five containers are needed by a homemaker who strives for beauty in her arrangements. A person who exhibits in flower shows needs even more and usually larger containers in order to compete with experts. A collection of containers should be acquired gradually because taste improves with experience and new styles often appear on the market. A homemaker should buy containers in harmony with the texture, color, scale, and style of furnishings in her own house.

Six basic containers that would probably be of most use to a homemaker are listed here.

A medium-sized, *low, round,* banded (around base) container of pale, grayed, warm-green pottery of fine texture.

A medium-sized, *low, oval,* banded, fine pottery container in white shading to green at the top or to the dominant color in owner's dishes for the dining-table centerpiece.

A *tall,* banded, pewter container with slightly curved sides, for cool-colored flowers to use without a stem holder.

A *tall,* banded, beige container with straight sides, for warm-colored flowers, to use without a stem holder.

An *urn* without handles in fine, pale, warm-gray pottery or white alabaster, for mass arrangements.

188

A *large, tall* (over one foot), leaf-green or light brown pottery jar for floor arrangements of foliage and large flowers.

A prospective buyer should analyze a container as she would any other art product, considering each one of the art elements in turn.

Form. The shape of a container must be well proportioned and subtle in its variations. Those that have a band or base effect made as a part of the container are preferable. The footed containers, too, are good looking unless the feet are so small and tapering that they appear out of scale. The compotes (on stems) are usually picturesque; they lift the plant materials and create space areas below the arrangements. Large, low, round, banded containers are useful for exhibition work; they serve as frames for the pictures composed in them. Tall and medium-sized containers that turn in at the top require no stem holders and are useful for quick home arrangements. Bottles of pleasing shape made of dark glass or stone are needed for line arrangements. Some free-form containers should be acquired also for variety. Silver wine coolers and punch bowls are useful for large formal tea arrangements. Pitchers, soup tureens, and other household receptacles that are well formed and suitable may be used for flower arrangements.

Color. Containers should, of course, be inconspicuous in color and should blend with flower materials. Some Oriental teachers say that containers should suggest the color of the earth from which the flowers grow. Beige, tan, brown, gray, leaf-green, olive green, chartreuse, grayed green, grayed yellow, grayed orange, grayed violet, silver, copper, bronze, and gilt are all suitable for containers. White is used only if there are white materials in the arrangement, or if the container stands on a white tablecloth. Black is used only if there are black materials in the composition, as black coal or burned sticks, or if it is part of a strictly neutral arrangement of white, gray, and black. The reason for these restrictions on black and white is that the container and the plant materials do not form a unit unless the color of the container is repeated in the plant materials.

Pattern. The decorative pattern on a container should usually be entirely missing, because the container must be less conspicuous than the flowers. Some arrangers use decorated period containers, especially the Victorian, to establish the mood or the period. It seems advisable, however, to profit by our additional knowledge of design and to avoid the mistakes that were made in the original periods.

Texture.   Containers are available in textures that suit the various flowers and foliage. Texture depends to a large extent on the material from which the container is made.

Glass is the most delicate texture to be found in containers; it is suitable for flowers like sweet peas and cosmos. Tall clear glass vases are almost impossible to use because the stems show and it is hard to control their placement. Leaf-green, brown, or dark violet glass is easier to use than the clear glass. A low glass container to match the table glassware is a useful investment. The stem holders in glass containers may be obscured by green or amber glass marbles or by dyed water, if the plant materials do not hide them.

Pottery containers of many shapes, colors, and textures are available, and come in a wide range of prices. Among the best containers are those that are hand-made by well-known potters. Some Oriental pottery is highly desirable for use as containers; the best of these are beautiful in form and finish and are without decoration. The dull glazes of these expensive products are highly preferable to the more common shiny finishes. Valuable pottery or porcelain containers should have an inner container, possibly tin foil, or an inner coat of paraffin wax to protect them; they should not hold water for long periods.

Inexpensive pottery containers may be procured at the dime stores but they must be selected with care. Some of these pottery pieces are satisfactory in form; it is regrettable that they are often too shiny, and those that are bluish-green are usually discordant with green leaves; however, they may be painted. Arrangers can easily learn to make their own pottery containers.

Metal containers are especially suitable for use with plant materials that have woody stems, and also with dry materials. Yellowish flowers and leaves look well in brass, orange flowers look well in copper, gray foliage and pink, lavender, and blue flowers look well in silver and pewter. Because of its intrinsic value a silver container suggests the use of elegant flowers like roses.

Baskets seem especially suitable for casual arrangements of rather simple materials. Oriental arrangers feel that baskets are suitable for all flowers and that since baskets are made of plant materials they are more harmonious with flowers than the much harder pottery or metal.

Bamboo containers too have that quality of naturalness that is pleasing. To the Occidental, however, they seem less elegant than fine pottery, porcelain, or silver.

Wooden containers seem especially harmonious with dry materials and other sturdy materials. Weathered wood, driftwood, or cypress knees may serve as containers for plant materials. Wood can also be so shaped and finished that it expresses elegance.

Natural containers are sometimes listed in flower show schedules. Among the best are a gourd, half a squash, an unhusked coconut, sea shells of all kinds, and driftwood.

The search for containers may be a life-long hobby that never loses its appeal. This search takes one to gift shops, department stores, museums, potters' studios, dime stores, second-hand stores, junk yards, and to the ocean and the mountains in our homeland and in far-off countries. Sometimes this hunting is a fascinating adventure and the rewards are rich.

Bases. Bases under containers are considered in flower show practice to be a part of the container. An arrangement in competition or on exhibition should usually be placed on a base, stand, slab, raft, or mat to raise it up, to make it seem more important, and also to provide transition between the container and the table. A white container looks weak indeed when placed directly on a white table in a flower show.

Wooden bases are used more than any others. Carved round Oriental bases of teakwood are generally available, and are usually fine in texture. Most of them are black, but they are easily painted some harmonious color like brown, gray, or green.

Larger round bases are made by painting or staining bread or cake boards. Rectangular and square slabs can be made by a woodworker to fit one's own containers. A cross section of a tree trunk, a stump, or a burl is often handsome, and the natural convolutions on the edges made an interesting effect. Artificial indentations of the edge of a slab from a tree or burl are unpleasant, however, because they are meaningless imitations of the real thing. Old weathered and worn flattish pieces of wood or heavy bark are suitable bases for driftwood arrangements.

Thin stone slabs or blocks can usually be obtained from a stone cutter who makes cemetery markers. Several slabs of different sizes may be used over one another to express dignity or some other thought.

PROBLEMS IN CONTAINERS
(Suggestions from which to choose)

1. Report on one of the world's producers of beautiful ceramic or glass products.
2. Report on an outstanding American potter.
3. Draw a page of containers copied from Oriental products.
4. Cut out shapes of small containers from colored paper. Mount the best on a page.
5. Make a small container of inexpensive clay.
6. With inexpensive oil paint, paint some containers and bottles a dull, soft, warm leaf-green.
7. Make a container from an old phonograph record by warming it slightly in the oven and bending up the edges.

FRIEZE OF CONTAINERS. A shelf in the author's dining room fits above the windows. The valance board extends an inch above the shelf and down far enough to conceal the mechanics of the Venetian blinds.

AN ARRANGER'S COLLECTION. These upper shelves of the floor-to-ceiling cupboard in the author's home were filled for this photograph. Usually, however, each aperture is treated as a unit; sometimes only one type of container is exhibited at a time. Of the containers pictured here, some are valuable, some cost about a dollar or less, and some are second-hand.

A POTTERY CONTAINER. Rocks conceal the stem holder in this natural canna arrangement. The leaves and flowers make a pleasing silhouette with voids of various shapes and sizes.

Chapter 21

MECHANICS OF FLOWER

ARRANGING

The arranging of flowers includes control of the mechanics involved. The most important articles, of course, are the container and the stem holder. Additional items that the arranger should have in her tool kit include clippers, scissors, wire cutters, knife, modeling clay, three weights of florists' wire, "twistems," green cord, Scotch tape, pins, paper clips, rubber bands, and dry hollow stems like poinsettia and bamboo. Some arrangers use other aids also; it is a matter of personal preference. Still another important aid is an automobile, containing buckets of water, an ax, saw, clippers, and an observant driver.

The *pin-point stem holder* is the best type for general use. These holders come in several sizes and shapes: round, oval, crescent, and rectangular. The large, heavy ones used for large arrangements need not be attached to the containers. The small and medium-sized stem holders must be fastened down with modeling clay or paraffin wax. If the inside of a container has a rounded bottom, it is first necessary to pour enough hot paraffin wax in it to get a flat surface. After it hardens, affix the stem holder with a little more hot wax.

When modeling clay is used to attach a stem holder in a container all factors must be perfectly dry: the container, the stem holder, the clay, and the arranger's hands. Small balls of clay are put under the edges of the stem holder, which is then settled firmly

195

into the container. For line arrangements, small pin-holders are best because they can be easily concealed. Only paraffin should be used in silver containers because some modeling clay stains silver and other metals.

For a mass arrangement to be made in an urn it is well to use two kinds of stem supports. A pin-point holder is attached to the bottom of the urn, and crushed chicken wire may be used above that. Sometimes it is possible to put a wire around the container near the top, stretch other wires across the top of the container, and attach these to the first wire to help control the flower placements. Wires that show when the arrangement is finished are cut away. Narrow strips of lead are also used inside the container in mass arrangements. They are wrapped around stems that lean over the edge of the container to hold them in place.

Hairpin stem holders that look like wire hairpins are useful for mass arrangements too. *Bird-cage stem holders* made over pin-point stem holders are sometimes useful, but they are apt to interfere with the positions of the flowers. Glass or pottery disks with holes in them for stems are nearly impossible to use in flower arrangements.

Tall containers may have a pin-point holder at the bottom and also some control at the rim. Lead strips that go around the stems, down into the container and over the edge are useful to hold materials in place at the rim. Scotch tape is also helpful, especially for S curves.

For stem support in a tall cylindrical container the Japanese use *two crossed sticks* that are cut a little longer than the diameter of the container and tied firmly together. They are forced into place a little way below the rim.

It is possible to use one strong central nandina foliage stem with its many smaller stems and leaves as a support for a mass flower arrangement. The nandina is impaled on a pin-point stem holder. The nandina leaves become a part of the finished picture; the many little cross stems hold the flowers in place (see page 210).

Some arrangers fill their tall vases with upright sword fern or cedar or juniper twigs. These are cut off an inch below the top of the container so that they do not show; they provide good support for flower stems.

Florists have plastic blocks capable of holding water that they use for stem support. Plastic foam is another useful material that makes a good support for woody stems. It can be painted a harmonizing color. Sometimes it is used as a substitute for a container, especially for Christmas decorations.

Wiring of flower stems and leaves in arrangements is usually permissible in flower shows, provided none of it shows. Sometimes a wire inserted into the center of a flower and down into the stem will support a weak neck and will allow the arranger to turn the face of the flower where she wants it to be. Aspidistra leaves can be controlled by putting a wire under Scotch tape along the midrib on the back of the leaf (see page 51).

Small stems like sweet peas that cannot stand alone on the stem holder are usually tied in little bunches of five or six. Sometimes a bit of strong stem is wired or tied to the end of a weak stem so that it can be impaled on the stem holder. A tall stem like gladiolus is sometimes reinforced at the base by placing one or more three-inch pieces of strong stem snugly against it on the stem holder. Some weak hollow stems are strengthened by inserting a short, solid stem like day-lily or aspidistra and tying it tightly. Stems that tend to split and curl up are controlled by wrapping and tying the ends with cord.

Concealing the stem holder is a troublesome part of making arrangements. It is no problem in a mass arrangement because the volume of material easily covers the stem holder. In a line arrangement, however, the design may suffer if extra leaves or flowers are used merely to cover the stem holder. If leaves are used for this purpose, do not place single separate leaves in flat horizontal positions because that effect is weak and unnatural. Instead, make little bunches of several leaves tied together so that they stand up vigorously on the stem holder.

Sand, black sand, bird-cage gravel, and pebbles are useful in hiding stem holders. Glass gravel is more elegant and colorful; glass marbles are also used. Water-worn and rounded rocks are successful for this purpose too; one should collect sets of 5 similar rocks of different sizes. Interesting bits of drift wood, fungi, and shells may also be used as foils. Anything that conceals stem holders, however, should be used subtly so that it becomes an integral part of the design (see page 194).

An expert arranger carefully hides all the mechanical aids, especially in flower shows where the work is on dress parade. Although the flower show judges keep their distance from the arrangements, the public has no such polite inhibitions.

FOR A COFFEE TABLE

Chapter 22

DIRECTIONS FOR MAKING FLOWER

ARRANGEMENTS

Detailed directions are given here for making five American flower arrangements and five adaptations of Japanese flower arrangements. In a general course in flower arrangement in the United States, however, there would probably be twenty or more American flower arrangements to one Japanese. The Japanese arrangements are described in detail here because few books in English contain all these directions.

PROBLEM I
How to Make a Sparse Foliage Arrangement

Plan an arrangement using three or five stems of ivy, iris, aspidistra, sword fern, barberry, ligustrum, 'eleagnus, new pine tips, yew, or sago palm.

1. Use a low round or oval container with a small pin-point holder attached off-center at the left. The size of the container depends on the size of the plant materials you will use.
2. Cut a strong stem or branch that is twice the width of the container plus its depth. Impale the stem on the rear of the stem holder. This is the primary placement.
3. Cut a stem that is a third shorter than the primary placement and impale it close to the left of the primary stem bending slightly forward and to the left.
4. Cut the third stem about a third the length of the primary stem

and impale it close to the right of the primary stem bending it forward and right. If your branches are broad you may not need any more stems; if so, omit the two additional stems described here.

5. Cut a stem that will reach forward well over the edge of the container at the right front and impale it close to the others on the stem holder.

6. Cut a short stem that will reach just over the edge of the container and point downward at the left front and impale it close to the others on the stem holder.

7. For emphasis at the focal area where the stems all meet add some more of the same leaves of a larger size or add one or more natural leaf rosettes like pittosporum or magnolia.

8. Adjust the stems so that the voids or spaces between the stems are all different.

PROBLEM II
How to Make a Line Arrangement
(See Chapter 13)

Plan an arrangement using three flowering branches of different lengths.

1. Choose a tall container that is harmonious with the plant material in scale, form, texture, and color.

2. Choose your branches carefully, the longest one should have definite character and distinction. The two secondary lines should follow the direction of the primary line. ____ a little longer than this.

3. Cut the primary branch twice the height of the container plus its depth.

4. Prune the branches if necessary to reveal their strength and beauty. Sometimes all the leaves and twigs that point downward should be removed because they counteract the upward growth movement.

5. Bend the branches if necessary to get graceful lines.

6. Place the main branch in the container so that it shows to its best advantage. Support it with lead strips that hook over the rim of the container at the back.

7. Place the shorter branches close to the long branch and hold them in place with the same lead strips. Arrange them so they will not detract from the leading branch.

8. Add one or two additional short stems of the same material at the rim if they are needed for weight.

9. Analyze your arrangement for proportion and balance. Snip out any-

thing that interferes with smooth, flowing rhythm. Look at your arrangement in a mirror.

PROBLEM III
How to Make a Modern Line-Mass Arrangement
(See Chapter 14)

Plan an arrangement of three sansevieria (or aspidistra) spikes, pink zinnias, and celosia (or some leaf rosettes).

1. Use a round gray container of medium height with a heavy pin-point stem holder attached in the center.
2. Cut the tallest sansevieria leaf about two and a half times the width of the container plus its depth. Impale it on the rear left part of the stem holder. Let its tip come over the middle of the container if possible.
3. Cut another sansevieria leaf about two inches shorter, impale it in front of the first leaf, and bend it toward the right.
4. Cut another sansevieria leaf about three inches shorter than the second leaf and impale it on the stem holder at the left of the other leaves with a void between their tips.
5. Place three, five, or more zinnias (or other strong, round flowers) against the lower right side of the spikes and at their base. Place some flowers back of the leaves also if there is room for them there.
6. Place the celosia low at the right hanging over the edge of the container, and pointing upward at the rim of the container on the left side of the arrangement. Add enough celosia to make a mass effect retaining some voids in the mass.
7. Natural leaf rosettes like magnolia or loquat may be substituted for the celosia in this design.

PROBLEM IV
How to Make a Large Symmetrical Stylized Mass Arrangement
(See Chapter 15)
*To be used in church, or on the refreshment table
at a formal reception, or for a formal dinner party*

1. Obtain a plain white urnlike container of fine quality.
2. Use some large-mesh pliable chicken wire and a large pin-point stem holder or some florists' plastic material for stem support.
3. Plan a bisymmetrical design suggesting a pyramid with open sides,

using light and dark blue delphinium for spikes, white carnations for transition in size, and white lilies at the center of interest.

4. Place the longest, strongest spike of dark blue delphinium high in the center, and one or two slightly shorter dark blue spikes in front of it to hide its stem.
5. Place long dark blue delphinium spikes of equal length pointing sideways and slightly downward on opposite sides of the center, add several slightly shorter dark blue spikes on and beside the long spikes.
6. Place many light blue delphinium spikes of varying lengths against the central placement and against the two low side placements until a mass effect is produced. This may take three dozen spikes.
7. Protect the large side voids, do not fill them.
8. If you need a deep, free-standing arrangement to be seen from the back too, add horizontal placements extending forward and backward from the center, like those at the sides, so that the whole design is like a flat wheel with four horizontal spokes and one spoke erect at the hub.
9. Place the low focal material, the white lilies, in position, after cutting their stems different lengths. Do not let the lilies suggest a sunken center.
10. Fill in the area around the lilies with white carnations, extending a row toward each spoke. Also, on each side of the focal area, add a separate row of white carnations curving downward.

PROBLEM V
How to Make a Dinner-Table Centerpiece
(See Chapter 16)

1. Use a low oval-shaped bowl or banded container, preferably white.
2. Fasten a long pin-point holder in it, using paraffin.
3. Plan a symmetrical arrangement with a diagonal center of interest on each side, using pink roses, pink larkspur, white iris, and sweet peas. Do not make it taller than fifteen inches above the table.
4. Tie the larkspur stems together in bunches of three. Tie the sweet peas in bunches of ten, so they will stand up on the stem holder.
5. Set up the larkspur like a fence down the length of the container in the center and extending far out and downward on each end. Leave some voids in the silhouette.
6. Place the pink roses low in a diagonal line at the center on one side of the arrangement. Fill in the same side with white iris of various lengths.

7. Place the white iris low in a diagonal line across the center on the other side of the arrangement. Fill in with sweet peas on this side only.
8. Keep the arrangement airy by having stems of different lengths and leaving sufficient voids.
9. If the arrangement seems too gentle and mild add to it about twenty iris leaves to make it lively. Let them radiate from the stem holder following the same direction as the flower stems.

ADAPTATIONS OF JAPANESE FLOWER ARRANGEMENTS

PROBLEM VI
How to Make a Formal Rikka Adaptation
(See Chapter 12)

Plan to use five different kinds of foliage representing Air, Earth, Fire, Wind, and Water, and flowers to represent frail Human Beings.

1. Use a plain, tall, dark, open-mouthed container, preferably an altar jar, or an usubata.
2. Fasten a heavy pin-point holder in the bottom of the jar with wax.
3. Cut six or seven bamboo sticks about the thickness of a fishing pole and about four or five inches taller than the part of the jar that holds the water, making some sticks longer than others. Have a joint near the bottom of each stick. If necessary coat the inside of each stem with melted paraffin wax.
4. Impale these sticks close together in the middle of the stem holder. Brace them with other bamboo sticks, some of which have been split. Add rocks for additional bracing if necessary.
5. Fill the hollow bamboo sticks with water. Each stick will hold the stem of a foliage branch or flowers.
6. Collect foliage branches that will face the arranger when in the required position: (1) a tall straight piece of English yew, (2) a cedar branch pointing upward and then downward and to the right, (3) a pepper tree branch, mimosa, asparagus-fern, or other airy foliage pointing to the right and slightly downward at the end, (4) a pine branch pointing upward and to the left, (5) a variegated privet branch pointing upward and slightly left, and some additional branches or twigs of all these types of foliage in case they are needed to fill out the composition.
7. Cut the branches as follows (add to these dimensions the length

needed inside the container): the central stalk of yew three times the height of the container, the cedar (lower right) two-thirds the length of the center stalk, the pine (lower left) two-thirds the length of the center stalk, the privet (upper left) three-quarters the length of the center stalk, the pepper (upper right) three-quarters the length of the center stalk. Cut the helper branches later, finding the length you need as you work.

8. Place the English yew, representing Air or Sky, upright in the exact center of the arrangement. If it appears skimpy place another shorter yew branch in front of it.

9. Place the cedar branch, representing Water, at the lower right side of the arrangement, pointing downward. Let several inches of bare branch show toward its base.

10. Place the pine branch, representing Earth or Origin, in the shortest bamboo stick, at the lower left side of the arrangement, pointing upward. Its base is opposite Water but lower down. Let the bare wood show at the base and elsewhere. Thin the needles and shorten them if necessary.

11. Place the variegated privet, representing Fire, pointing upward at the left of the central branch and nearer to it than to Earth. Place one or two shorter stems of privet along its upper side if necessary.

12. Place the pepper foliage, representing Wind, near the upper right side of the central branch, pointing upward but with its end pointing downward, however, leaving a large void between Wind and Water. Use sufficient helpers for the necessary volume.

13. Place the flowers along the lower portion of the central stalk facing forward near the base of Fire and Wind, but not below Earth or Water. A few lilies or gladiolus or other strong flowers may be used.

14. Add extra upright yew foliage just above the bamboo stem holders to broaden the center. Do not cover the bamboo holders, which represent the trunk of a tree, possibly the Tree of Life.

15. Display the arrangement on the floor or on a low table.

PROBLEM VII
How to Make a Classical Adaptation
(See Chapter 12)

Plan a right-handed arrangement consisting of Heaven, Man, and Earth, with four helpers. (In a right-handed arrangement Heaven and Earth turn to the right.)

1. Use any plain, dark, medium-height or tall container; however, traditional containers are preferred.

2. Use a finger-sized freshly cut forked or split stick as a stem holder. Cut it a little longer than the diameter of the container.

3. Place the forked stick inside the container horizontally about two inches below the rim with the forked end at the center in the rear. The stem holder may show in a classical Japanese arrangement.

4. Use materials that turn their best side to you when placed in a right-handed arrangement. For the Heaven line get a long slender branch that curves to the right if possible, or a long flower stem with a bud at the end. For Man get a branch or flower of the same material as Heaven. Also get some shorter materials of the same kind for helpers. The Earth line may be the same as H and M or it may be different, it may consist of flowers. If H and M and E are all flowerless, you might well add flowers as helpers in front of H and between H and E.

5. Cut your materials so that the part above the container's rim measures as follows: Heaven should be twice the height of the container, Man two-thirds the height of Heaven, and Earth one-third the height of Heaven. Cut the helpers as you use them; let no two lines be equal in length.

6. Prune your materials. Remove all flowers, leaves and twigs that do not count. Remove most of the downward-pointing leaves or twigs on M and E. Let some bare branch sections show to express strength.

7. Bend your materials. If possible bend the H line in a bow-like curve that points right. Bend M so it follows H but leans to the left about four inches above the rim, keeping the tip up. Bend E sharply to the right about two inches above the rim, keeping the tip up.

8. Place all your stems in the crotch of the forked stick stem holder, allowing them to rest on the bottom or against the side of the container. First place Earth, so that it points to your right shoulder, pressing it tightly into the crotch of the stick, then place Earth's helpers behind it. Second, place Heaven and its helper tightly against the back of Earth and its helpers. The concave side of H is to the right, its tip is directly over its base. Third, place Man tightly against the other stems as far left as possible, then place its helper next to it on its right. Bend them to the left. Let Man point upward and forward with its tip turned toward Heaven.

9. Now place a straight stick horizontally close behind all the stems of the arrangement to hold them firmly. Sometimes one or two extra short stems are added to the group of stems if they seem loose in the stem holder.

10. To "polish" your arrangement, adjust the materials so that the

effect is smooth. The three main groups—H, M, and E—should be distinct; any leaves or flowers that interfere or are confusing should be removed. If the arrangement seems too sparse, add some more helpers.

11. Place your arrangement against a plain background, about at the eye level of a seated person.

PROBLEM VIII
How to Make a Nageire Adaptation
(See Chapter 12)

Plan a left-handed "over-the-cliff" design to be placed above the eye level.

1. Use a tall, plain container.
2. Use some finger-sized sticks for stem holders. A long lead strip may also be used for control at the rim. Don't stuff your container with fern or evergreen for stem control, because some water should show when seen from above.
3. Look for a long, leaning, interesting branch or flower stem for the Man line that will show its better side when leaning to the right. Procure two shorter, possibly thicker, lines of different lengths for Heaven and Earth.
4. Prune off the surplus leaves, twigs, or flowers. Remove or bend any parallel or right-angled twigs.
5. Tie a stick across the end of the long branch. Force it into the container. Let the branch lean over the edge of the container to the right. If placed on the mantel it may hang below the container. This is usually called the Man line.
6. Place the Heaven and Earth lines so as to make a triangle with Man. The H line is taller than E; place it between M and E—it may lean slightly but still point upward. Use sticks to hold the M and E in place.
7. Cover most, but not all, of the rim from the front view.
8. Analyze your arrangement. If it lacks interest add a few flowers and buds between the two short branches.
9. Place your arrangement off-center on a shelf or cabinet so that the larger space is to the left.

PROBLEM IX
How to Make a Flower Moribana Adaptation
(See Chapter 12)

Plan a right-handed arrangement using nine stems. Reverse the positions given here if you want a left-handed arrangement.

1. Use a plain, low, rounded or oval container.
2. Fasten the pin-point holder with clay or paraffin wax in the left front quarter of your container.
3. Use flowers for the Earth group.
4. Use different flowers or foliage for the Heaven and Man groups.
5. Cut the Heaven line so that its length is about one and one-half times the diameter of the container or less. Cut two slightly shorter helpers of different lengths.
6. Cut the Man line one-quarter shorter than H. Cut two shorter helpers for M.
7. Cut the Earth line one-quarter shorter than M. Cut two shorter helpers for E.
8. Check your material and see that no two lines are the same length.
9. Prune away surplus leaves and twigs.
10. Impale the Heaven group at the rear of the stem holder, with the longer helper behind and left of H and the shorter helper in front slightly to the right, making a triangle. Curve all the tips toward the right if possible. Keep the tip of H over its base, if that is not too difficult.
11. Impale the Man group on the left part of the stem holder; bend it to the left and then upward. Man is the farthest out, the longer helper is next and the shorter helper forward, making a triangle of the Man group. Turn all stems and tips in the same directions as the H group.
12. Impale the Earth group on the right front part of the stem holder and point it toward your right shoulder. Earth is the farthest out; it usually extends forward over the edge of the container. The shorter helper is placed next to E; it is the lowest point in the arrangement. The longer helper is placed next to Heaven. The Earth group also makes a triangle. This group helps to cover the stem holder.
13. If the stem holder is still exposed, some foliage, moss, pebbles, or rocks may be carefully used to conceal it.
14. Check the arrangement to see that the total effect is a triangle from the front view and also from above. Prune out any leaves that prevent easy recognition of the H, M and E groups.

15. Add more material if you need it.

16. Think about your arrangement and what you are trying to express with it, and give it a seasonal name.

The flower Moribana described above was to be made in the forward part of a container. The stem holder may instead be located off-center in the rear of the container. Then the proportions and positions may be different from the forward arrangement. Man then may be the length of the diameter of the container; Heaven may be about two-thirds of the diameter and Earth one-third of the diameter. In the rear arrangement Man usually points across the empty part of the container, H is upright and E is horizontal, and points in the opposite direction from M.

PROBLEM X
How to Make a Landscape Moribana Adaptation
(See Chapter 12)

Plan a left-handed, divided, water-viewing composition.

1. Use a low rectangular container of wood, dark metal, or dark pottery.

2. Attach the pin-point stem holders as follows: a small one very close to the rear right corner for a helper, a larger one in front and left of it for Heaven, a smaller one in front of H and slightly toward center for Man, and a small one in the front left corner for the Earth group.

3. Use an interesting leaning Heaven branch with small leaves from a tree or a shrub. Cut it about the length of the container. Prune the lower part so that it looks like a tree trunk. Use a separate stick for a tree trunk if you want a thicker one.

4. Impale the Heaven line at the back of the large stem holder; let it point diagonally across the container to the opposite (left front) corner.

5. Cut a Man line of the same foliage one-third shorter than H.

6. Place M on its own stem holder pointing toward your right shoulder; its tip should stand higher than the leaning Heaven.

7. Use some foliage or grasses and water-worn stones to make the three levels in the Earth group.

8. Place the Earth group at the left front corner diagonally opposite the base of the larger group in a triangle effect. Make it less than half the height of the taller group.

9. Check your composition to see that the highest point of each group is toward the outside, so that the effect of an interior valley is obtained.

10. Fill in the arrangement if it is sparse, placing helpers in front of and back of H and M.
11. Have irregular heights and depths in your landscape.
12. Add a small figurine that is in scale if it helps the effect. If necessary paint it so that it blends into the landscape.
13. Consider the effect you have produced; perhaps it reminds you of a natural scene that you know. Think of what it expresses and give it a name.

A FIGURINE AS A CENTER OF INTEREST. This Oriental goddess expresses charm and intelligence. The fragrant narcissi are right in scale. The horizontals at the base strengthen the design.

212

PART VIII

Exhibiting and Judging

Some Flower Show Classes
Flower Arrangements by Juniors
Judging Arrangements in Flower Shows

Chapter 23

SOME FLOWER SHOW CLASSES

MODERN FLOWER ARRANGEMENTS

Modern arrangements are in accord with modern architecture, painting, sculpture, and industrial arts, all developments of the twentieth century. In design they are clean-cut, stylized, and sometimes geometric. They are often large, stark, dramatic, and masculine; they feature form and texture. In color they are neutral or bold, never weak.

Containers for modern arrangements are absolutely plain, often geometric in shape, and usually neutral or subdued in color.

Modern arrangements require *plant materials* that are fairly large, clean-cut in form, and controllable in placement; filler materials are not used. Exotic and unusual materials are desirable. The flowers and leaves of callas, birds-of-paradise, anthuriums, gladiolus, amaryllis, and bananas are among the many materials suitable for modern flower arrangements.

STYLIZED FLOWER ARRANGEMENTS

A stylized arrangement may be a line, line-mass, or mass arrangement. Stylized means somewhat the same as the term "conventionalized" used to mean in regard to design. It is the opposite of free or natural, also the opposite of a hit-or-miss effect. All "modern" arrangements are highly stylized. The work of the designer is obvious in them because the material is plainly organized into a deliberate design. The segregation of both colors and materials required

214

by stylization brings out the beauty of each individual piece of plant material.

Practice in making stylized arrangements will be found useful to all who wish to work artistically with plant materials. The modern furnishings prevalent today call for this type of decoration. In flower shows most arrangements are stylized to some extent.

NATURAL FLOWER ARRANGEMENTS

A natural or naturalistic arrangement is one that appears as if the arranger has not tampered with it in any way. Only plant material that has beauty of design within itself should be used in this fashion. In a natural arrangement the sensitive artist has a chance to portray the essence of this one plant, for it is usually shown alone. Often a single branch, spray, or stalk is set up in a suitable plain container all by itself, although sometimes more of the same material is added for balance and weight. For example, a branch from an apple tree or a hydrangea bush, or a stalk of Easter lilies or celosia may have enough beauty of its own, without any arranging, if it is carefully selected and shown to advantage. Some pruning may be done to produce the effect desired. Natural arrangements may be either line or mass types depending on the density of the plant material.

These natural placements may well be called arrangements even though little is done to them, for fine taste is necessary in selecting and presenting the material. Judges should be warned not to look for focal areas in natural arrangements but to look for over-all rhythm and natural beauty.

Many horticulturists, naturalists, and artists prefer natural to stylized arrangements.

COMPOSITIONS WITH ACCESSORIES

In flower show language an accessory is anything used with or within a flower arrangement that is not fresh-cut plant material, except of course the container, the base, and the gravel, sand, or ground cork that may be used to conceal the stem holder. An accessory may be a figurine, a rock, fruit, piece of driftwood, a small separate arrangement, or any one of a great number of other things.

Formerly some flower show leaders arbitrarily decided that the use of an accessory with or within an arrangement makes it a "Composition." It would indeed be regrettable if that term "Composition," with its clear meaning in all the arts for centuries past, were to have such restricted meaning in the art of flower arrangement. "Composition" and "arrangement" are practically synonymous terms.

Figurines are the most used of the accessories. No doubt more arrangements have been ruined by figurines than by anything else. These small sculptures, usually of human beings or animals, should not be used in flower compositions unless they are absolutely necessary to express the theme or to complete the design.

In the first place, the figurines themselves should have excellence in design, color, and texture. Shiny, humorous animals, frilly dolls, ballet dancers, and period ladies are entirely out of place as accessories. Hand-make primitive wood carvings or contemporary sculptors' products are among the best figurines available. Most figurines are too small in scale to look well in flower compositions. Some arrangers make their own figurines from clay or wood. Any figurine can be painted to fit a color scheme and the paint removed later, if desired.

In the home a figurine may be used with very little plant material, even only one sprig of foliage. In a flower show, however, the plant materials should generally dominate. The schedule sometimes specifies which is to be featured, figurine or flowers.

In a floral composition a figurine may be placed at the core of the arrangement, with the plant materials organized around it. In this position the figurine usually dominates.

On the other hand, a figurine may be placed away from the main floral grouping. In such a case the figure should usually face into the picture, that is, look toward the arrangement, in order to connect the two parts. The lines of the floral material should usually reach toward the figurine, which should carry on the same rhythm of line as the plant material. A single base under the figurine and plant materials is necessary to hold them together as a unit and prevent their being two separate focal areas.

When two figurines are used together it is sometimes well to raise one of them on a block to avoid a static horizontal effect. A figurine of a dressed person or a land creature should not stand in the water in a container.

PAIRS OF ARRANGEMENTS

Pairs of arrangements make an interesting class in a flower show. A pair may be alike or may be related by similar containers or the same plant materials. Identical pairs are often used in church or on a lecture platform. A pair of arrangements may be used at home on the mantel shelf, on twin tables, or on the dining table.

A pair of arrangements can not be expected to look exactly alike because flowers are not alike. Identical but reversed asymmetrical pairs are more subtle than twin pairs; they may point toward one another, or to a central object standing between them. A pair may be different in size too, just as a man and his wife are a pair but are different in size. Mother-and-daughter arrangements which are almost alike except in size are pleasing variations of the pair idea.

MINIATURE ARRANGEMENTS

Miniature arrangements are hard to make and are almost impossible to use in a home. They are out of scale with human beings and their dwellings. Six- or eight-inch miniatures are highly preferable to the three-inch arrangements that are sometimes exhibited in flower shows.

The most important restriction in miniatures is scale; no leaf or flower should be larger than about one-third of the container. Single florets from a group like hydrangea blossoms should not be used. The effect sought is that of a complete arrangement to which all the design principles apply. Line and line-mass arrangements are more effective than mass in miniatures or small arrangements. Miniatures made of dry materials are often used in doll houses.

CORSAGES

Beauty, fitness, and technical quality are requirements in a corsage. The skillful arranger is able to make the corsage light in weight and yet wrap each stem to protect the garment on which it is worn and also to prolong the life of the flowers.

The design principles apply to a corsage; there should be a center of interest and some less important areas. The flowers should be in scale with one another and with the ribbon, being much more important than the ribbon.

The texture of a corsage affects its suitability. Certain delicate flowers look best in dressy corsages. Hardy flowers belong in corsages for street or suit wear. In the fall and winter corsages of dry materials like nuts, seed pods, leaves, and grain are seasonal and suitable on winter dresses, suits, and coats.

Good books are available on corsage-making and expert class instruction is available in some places. In flower shows corsages may be exhibited attached to the branches of a leafless tree or to a wall board, or to other devices, or placed on high tables. A corsage may be put in a cellophane envelope with stiff backing to protect it when it is being exhibited or transported.

TABLE SETTINGS

One of the most popular sections of a flower show is the table settings. It is considered of such importance that often a tricolor award is given in the tables section alone. Classes range from coffee tables to formal dinner tables. In a show a table should be set up for one particular course with all items in place except silverware and food.

A *theme or an idea* is a requirement in many of the table-setting classes. A theme can be expressed through the design, color, and texture of every article on the table. A theme such as Grandma's birthday would produce a very different result from a Fourth-of-July theme.

Pattern is the most important element in a table setting. All the patterns on the chinaware, glassware, silverware, and tablecloth should belong to the same period of decorative art. The patterns should usually have similar motifs, such as stars, roses, or ivy leaves, and should be compatible in size or scale. The total amount of patterned and plain surfaces should be planned; the plain areas should be greater than the patterned areas. The background of the table setting is the cloth; a plain cloth makes a better background than a decorated one. Lace cloths can never serve as quiet backgrounds. The entire table setting should present a beautiful pattern of well distributed articles against the ultimate background, the table top.

Color harmony is the same in a table setting as elsewhere: one color should dominate. A white cloth or white mats call for some white flowers. Silverware looks better with cool colors than with warm; brass-colored flatware looks better with warm colors than with cool. The floral centerpiece usually includes all the colors used anywhere on the table.

Texture harmony is important, too, where such a variety of things is assembled. Fine linen, porcelain, glassware, silverware, and fine flowers are consistent on a fine wood table. Pewter goblets, pottery plates, and bone-handled flatware are harmonious and suitable for a very informal place or occasion.

The *floral decoration* in a table setting may be one centerpiece or multiple arrangements. A very long table may have diagonal effects to break its length. The decoration may be at one or both ends of a rectangular table with the place settings at the sides of the table. A centerpiece should not take up too much space; a reasonable amount is the central fifth of a rectangular table. In height the centerpiece should be below the eye level of the seated diners, except for a formal dinner or for buffet service.

Fruit, vegetable, and foliage table decorations are attractive and functional for home use and should be shown in flower shows. These arrangements should be restrained in variety and color; all should have upstanding foliage to provide height. They are described further on page 172.

Plant materials used on tables should be scrupulously clean and free from blemishes. Strongly scented flowers are objectionable to some persons and may be considered a demerit in a flower show competition. Flowers should be in water in a table setting in a flower show unless they are of a kind that will survive equally well without water.

Candle light makes a pleasant atmosphere for a meal and candles usually add needed height to table decorations. They are not used for daytime tables, however, except for a wedding table or a Christmas dinner table. In a flower show it is customary to char all candle wicks used in table settings. White candles are usually appropriate, but colored candles may enhance a color scheme with lively accents. Candlesticks should be tall so that the flame would be above the eyes of the seated diners.

A *bridge-table luncheon arrangement* should be low and small since space must be allowed for four place settings. Proper scale is important: no large flowers should be used. The arrangement must be free-standing, presentable from all sides and from above. Four corsages for the players might well constitute the centerpiece.

An arrangement for a *buffet supper table* is usually large, tall, and free-standing if the table stands away from the wall. It may well be informal and asymmetrical, since such suppers are informal. To emphasize informality in the table equipment the colors may be exciting, the textures bold, and the design unusual.

A *formal dinner-table setting* in a flower show should conform to the definition of such a table in the accepted books on table setting. Silverware is not usually allowed in a show, but the fine chinaware, glassware, linen, centerpiece, and other beautiful accessories are sufficient to carry out the formal effect. The centerpiece should be elegant and large and impressive for a formal dinner party.

An *every-day table setting* for a busy mother should be exhibited in flower shows. Since it should be practical and functional, plastic mats and paper napkins should be required. The floral decoration should be made of long-lasting foliage such as Japanese yew or sasanqua, with a focal area of temporary flowers.

The *analysis* of a table setting may be based on the *art principles*. For example: How is the *proportion* of the centerpiece in relation to the whole table? Does one end of the table *balance* the other end in weight? Is the centerpiece *dominant* or are the dishes and the cloth so full of pattern that the centerpiece is obscured? Is there pleasing *rhythm* in the whole setting? Are there some tall things on the table to lift the eyes and give *third dimension?* These questions should be applied to table settings both at home and in flower shows.

PROBLEMS
(Suggestions from which to choose)

1. Make a natural arrangement using plant material with interesting lines (see page 138).
2. Make a modern arrangement using large separate leaves overlapping one another. Use a large flower for the focal point. If you have no large flower, make a substitute by pinning (with common pins) small colored leaves round and round the end of a carrot.
3. Make a composition using a figurine at the core (see page 7).
4. Make a horizontal arrangement including some weathered wood and foliage.
5. Make a six-inch (or less) miniature of fresh or dry materials. Use tweezers for ease in handling (see page 238).
6. Make corsages under the direction of an experienced amateur, possibly a garden club member.
7. Make a fruit arrangement for a buffet supper, suitable for a flower show.
8. Make the floral centerpiece for the tea table for some function.
9. Make an arrangement suitable for a man's desk.

Chapter 24

FLOWER ARRANGEMENTS

BY JUNIORS

The purpose of having young people make flower arrangements is not to turn out finished products; it is to help children realize that this is an art in which they may participate, to give them a chance to express themselves, and to encourage them to make the home or schoolroom more attractive.

The Junior division in a flower show is of special interest, but too often some of the arrangements are not expressive of childhood. Junior arrangements should appear fresh, natural, casual, and spontaneous; any labored effects should be avoided. Children's work should not look like the work of adults; juniors should not try to copy those popular standardized, sophisticated arrangements like S-curves, crescents, or fan shapes that are made by many trained arrangers. Children should be encouraged to *express themselves* in flower arranging as they do in painting. Extreme originality, imagination, and experimentation should be the objectives. Simple materials, simply arranged, are expressive of childhood. A little fern in its own bit of surrounding moss expresses a child's love of nature.

In judging junior arrangements in flower shows the scale of points should be different from the ones used for adult arrangements. The following scale might be tried for some junior classes in flower arrangement.

224

Conforming to schedule _____ 15
Naturalness (non-stylization) _____ 15
Originality _____ 15
Simplicity (uncluttered quality) _____ 15
Design (balance, proportion, rhythm) _____ 20
Color _____ 10
Condition _____ 10
                                         ———
                                         100

Young people should be taught the proper care of plant materials. They should learn to cut flowers and foliage after sunset or before sunrise and to place them in deep water in a cool place for a few hours or overnight. They should understand how to be responsible for their arrangements, changing the water and rearranging and discarding the flowers at the proper time.

Wild flowers are of special interest to children. They should not be cut unless they can be placed in water immediately. Juniors should learn that it is antisocial to pick the wild flowers along the highways where motorists could enjoy them, and that some flowers must be left for seed wherever any are picked. They should also know which flowers are scarce and are protected by law in their own and neighboring states.

Junior arrangers should be separated into at least two divisions, those of elementary school age and those of junior high school age, because of the differences in the abilities and interests of the two groups.

Elementary School Children's Arrangements. These arrangements should appear especially simple. Arrangements that are easily made without much mechanical help should be demonstrated for small children. Miniatures, because of their intricacy and small size, should not be taught to small children.

Bottle arrangements are easy for small children; they may be made in dark-colored glass bottles. Two or three long stalks of plant material are usually all that can be inserted through the neck of a bottle. Children can easily learn to cut each stem a different length. They can also learn that it looks better to have more plant materials than bottle. Vines or curving stems look especially well in bottles with a few head flowers placed near the rim.

Drinking glass arrangements are often made by children who have no other containers available; leaf-green glasses are preferable to others. Sometimes children place just a short-stemmed rose or two in a glass; they should be taught to add a twig of foliage, as pittosporum, maple, or oak to help hold roses up, and to add some iris leaves or other spikes to give height. A diagonal arrangement can also be made in a glass without a stem holder by using plant materials that lean naturally. They lean on the rim for support, with their stems against the opposite side of the bottom of the glass.

Low saucer arrangements are also suitable for children to make. Even a primary-age child can learn to place a small, dry pin-point stem holder off-center in a plain, deep, dry saucer using dry modeling clay to fasten the holder down with dry hands. An easy saucer arrangement can be made from a low rosette of hydrangea leaves and a few short-stemmed flowers held together with a rubber band. Five or six short-stemmed day-lilies in a small chartreuse dish on the breakfast table might be the daily contribution of a child. Large buds could be picked a day ahead so that the family could watch them open at breakfast time.

Weed and grass arrangements are especially suitable for children, and such materials are usually available. Arrangements made from them should never be stylized but should look perfectly natural. Several materials may be combined, but the effect should be sparse. Containers for weeds should be plain and dull, suggesting the earth.

Evergreen foliage arrangements are satisfactory for children because they hold up well. Pine, cedar, juniper, arborvitae, sasanqua, magnolia, and loquat are among the many that are suitable. A few sturdy flowers like marigolds, calendulas, or zinnias may be added for color. A pottery or metal container about the size of a quart milk bottle is convenient for foliage arrangements.

Junior High School Students' Flower Arrangements. Several arrangements are considered here that might appeal to the interest of junior high students and are not too difficult for them. Students of this age may prefer to attempt to make arrangements like those they see in adult flower shows, but they should not be encouraged to do so.

A *patio arrangement* to accompany an outdoor meal may be made of some strong foliage such as pine, and two or three kinds of fruit. The fruit should be of different shapes and sizes. The container should not be entirely filled with fruit, since contrast is necessary. More information about fruit and vegetable arrangements appears on pages 172 and 173.

A *coffee table arrangement* for the living room is a suitable project for a young girl. It can be made in a shell, a green glass ashtray, or some other small container, with a pin-point stem holder attached in the center. The arrangement must be low and should look pretty from above and from the sides too. Any head flowers of medium size with some standing leaves at one side are pleasing. See page 198.

A *tussy-mussy arrangement* for a small table is a pleasant note, especially in a period home. It is made of fragrant flowers, if possible, and is usually held in the hand while being assembled. A round flower like a small rose, camellia, gardenia, aster, or carnation is surrounded by a circle of darker flowers like sweet peas, around which is placed another concentric circle of lighter flowers, around which is placed a circle of perfect ivy or geranium leaves. A string or rubber band is used to hold it all in place. The stems are trimmed to the same length. A paper lace doily may be placed under the circle of leaves. The tussy-mussy stems fit nicely into a small tin sausage can which has been sanded or painted white or leaf-green.

Corsages can be made by junior high school girls. The juniors should ask an experienced garden club member to teach them the fundamentals of corsage making. Perfection in technique is not necessary at this age. The emphasis should be on the flowers and the design; very little ribbon need be used. Texture combinations like a frilly carnation with an edge of curly parsley are interesting and effective. At Christmas time, attractive corsages can be made to wear with school clothes.

An arrangement made on a large coat button provides an opportunity for an altruistic project, because these tiny arrangements are suitable as gifts for bedridden persons such as patients in veterans' hospitals. They can be made of small-leaved succulent rosettes, such as hen-and-chickens, and succulent spikes, all sewed fast onto the button. A drop of water once a week will keep them alive.

A *dry arrangement* for her own room should interest a junior arranger. Such arrangements may lead to the wish to grow some everlasting and cockscomb. A girl might like to have her dry arrangement in a pottery or metal container. A boy might like one too, in half an unhusked coconut or in a container that he has made in wood-working class. Wet sand makes a satisfactory stem holder for a dry arrangement in any container. Three kinds of dry materials are enough for variety. Hunting dry seed pods makes an interesting autumn expedition.

A *dry framed arrangement* may be made of pressed flowers and leaves in a picture frame. A three-dimensional arrangement of seed pods and dry leaves may be placed in a deeper frame, covered with glass and hung on the wall. The dry materials are usually arranged as a group with stems together, naturally without a container. Materials may be glued in place. One material should dominate; sizes and shapes should vary. Plain frames are most suitable, and can usually be obtained at the dime stores.

A *driftwood arrangement* for home use needs very little plant material with it. In a flower show, however, the living plant material usually dominates in quantity. The driftwood should have interesting lines and masses and should be well weathered or polished. It usually looks best in an informal place like a patio or a sun room or game room. Any sturdy flowers or foliage are suitable with it, if they follow the same lines that are already present in the driftwood. Juniors of camping age should learn to appreciate sculptural form in weathered wood, so that they can collect good specimens. See page 175 for more about driftwood.

A *landscape composition* in three dimensions is usually interesting to juniors. It can be made in a small tray, a plate, or a bowl to stand on a table or in a niche, or it can be made in a deep frame and hung on the wall. It should show only a small detail of a natural landscape, such as a tree, a rock, a bush, and perhaps a figurine. The effect becomes spotty and confused if the tray is large and many separated objects are placed in it. Correct scale must be observed. See page 128 for further information about three-dimensional landscapes.

Blueprint pictures of flowers and leaves may prove interesting to junior high school boys and girls. The blueprints are easily made: lay a few flowers or leaves, usually with stems together, as flat as possible on unused blueprint paper, cover it with glass, clamp it firmly, expose it to sunlight or other strong light. Then wash and dry the paper, and you have the silhouetted picture. Flowers of distinctive form like columbine, bleeding heart, nasturtium, forget-me-not, lily-of-the-valley, and daisy are suitable, as are milkweed pods and seeds, wisteria vines and flowers, ferns, Hercules club leaves, buckeye leaves and spikes, and maple leaves and racemes. These blueprints may be mounted and used as wall decorations.

A *flower show* of junior arrangements may be staged by school children or by outside groups. *The Handbook for Flower Shows,* published by the National Council of State Garden Clubs, is an excellent guide in standard procedures. The flower show chairman, schedule committee, staging committee, entry committee, classification committee, and dismantling committee make a workable organization. The staging committee should understand that no decorations are desirable in the show room since the flower arrangements should have no competition. Light gray is the best color to use for backgrounds and for table tops.

PROBLEMS IN JUNIOR FLOWER ARRANGEMENT
(Suggestions from which to choose)

1. Make an arrangement for your teacher's desk, using some foliage and some flowers in a plain container.
2. Make an arrangement that shows that the wind is blowing. Give the arrangement a name.
3. Make an arrangement suitable for the breakfast table on a pin-point stem holder. Set it in a container that you have made of heavy metal foil.
4. Make an arrangement in a plain green cup and saucer. Place the tallest part and the biggest flower near the handle.

Chapter 25

JUDGING ARRANGEMENTS
IN FLOWER SHOWS

Most of the flower shows of today have competitive classes to be judged. Exhibitors rightly expect that the judging will be done by experts; however, there are not usually enough experts to supply the demand for them.

National Council of State Garden Clubs has met the problem wisely by planning comprehensive courses in flower show judging that are now being taught in nearly all the states. National Council gives an *Accredited Flower Show Judges' Certificate* to any member who attends a total of ten days of special lectures by experts, does the extensive required reading, passes examinations on both the lectures and reading, wins five blue ribbons, and judges in five standard flower shows. There are now several thousand Accredited Flower Show Judges in the United States. Their knowledge has improved flower shows and flower show judging to a remarkable extent.

In addition to the judges who are accredited by National Council there are many plant growers and specialists who are excellent judges of horticulture. College professors of horticulture, landscape design, and art are, of course, among the superior judges in their special fields. Anyone who is interested in becoming a judge of flower arrangements should take courses in the subject and also in art, and should read the excellent books that are available on Oriental and Occidental arrangements.

A flower show judge should have certain qualifications: experience, knowledge, fairness, courage, patience, courtesy, and tact. Cooperation with other judges and with the tense, busy show officials is of utmost importance. In analyzing flower arrangements judges should learn to look for beauty instead of flaws. They should strive to understand the idea and the mood that the arranger has tried to express.

ANALYSIS AND POINT SCORING

Judges and exhibitors of flower arrangements must understand perfectly how to analyze and point score arrangements in order to do their work well. When judges point score flower arrangements they analyze more fairly and accurately than they otherwise could. The use of a scale of points necessitates painstaking evaluation of the merits of an arrangement. In this process the personal tastes or prejudices of a judge are mitigated.

Point judging is slower than ordinary judging; therefore it is usually impossible to point judge all the arrangements in a flower show. As much point scoring should be done, however, as time allows. The most important classes may be fully point scored, or, if the time is limited, the four best arrangements in each class may be point scored. Where there is close competition, point scoring is necessary.

Judges should sign the point-scoring cards they have used, and these may be displayed beside the arrangements for the benefit of the public. This procedure makes a judge feel his or her responsibility strongly; it is conducive to careful, impartial judging.

Exhibitors, too, should know point scoring. They should study the scales of points to be used in the flower show classes in which they are exhibiting. The scales are usually published in the schedule of the show.

In analyzing and point scoring a flower arrangement the same factors that apply to the analysis of a painting or a piece of sculpture are considered. The elements of art—color, texture, line, form, and pattern—and the principles of art or design—proportion, balance, dominance, rhythm, and transition—have the same meaning in

EXHIBITING AND JUDGING

flower arrangement as in the other arts. Although transition may be considered to be a part of rhythm, it is included here because of its importance in flower arrangement.

SCALES OF POINTS

While judging in a flower show there is not sufficient time for judges to analyze arrangements in complete detail, applying to them all the principles and elements of art, and other considerations too. Therefore brief workable lists of qualities have come into general use at flower shows. These qualities are not considered to be equally important; their comparative values may be stated in a scale of points as follows:

SCALE OF POINTS FOR JUDGING A FLOWER ARRANGEMENT

Expressiveness (or Suitability)		15
Color		20
Design		25
Proportion	5	
Balance	5	
Dominance	5	
Rhythm	5	
Transition	5	
Texture		10
Originality		10
Distinction		10
Condition		10
Total		100

The above scale of points has proved useful to the author in teaching flower arrangement in college classes. This scale may be varied to suit special features or special kinds of arrangements. The term *pattern* should be added to a scale used for judging table settings. *Expressiveness* should always be used in a scale for judging arrangements with themes. *Distinction* is usually included in scales of points for use in advanced shows.

Special classes call for higher points in some items. *Theme* might rate 40 points in an interpretative class open to judges only. *Color* might be worth 40 points in a class calling for a special color scheme. *True to period* could even be worth 50 points in a class calling for a period arrangement.

Many different scales of points have been published. Various plant societies publish the scales that they prefer. Most federated garden clubs use the scales of points recommended in National Council's *Handbook for Flower Shows*.

A *standard method* of giving awards is recommended by the National Council of State Garden Clubs. In each class only one first (blue), one second (red), and one third (yellow) are given. As many honorable mentions (white) as are deserved may be given. Unless this method of making awards is followed, a flower show is not considered to be a *standard show*. In advanced shows usually the blue ribbon winner must score above 90, the red ribbon above 85, and the yellow ribbon above 80. In some classes all three ribbon winners may happen to score above 90. In other classes possibly no blue ribbon is given because there are no scores of 90 or better. For complete information about awards and other customary flower show practices see the *Handbook for Flower Shows*, published by the National Council of State Garden Clubs, Inc., 160 Central Park South, New York 19, N. Y.

Flower show judges are very fortunate in that they are able to perform their community service in this interesting and rewarding way. They have the pleasure of working with flowers, which are among the most beautiful products of this earth, and they are participating in the development of an important and democratic form of art, American flower arrangement.

FIRST PLACE WINNER. Score about 94. Its only demerit is that the roses are too close together.

VERTICAL ARRANGEMENTS IN COMPETITION
WITH THE ONE ON THE OPPOSITE PAGE

THIRD PLACE WINNER
Score about 78.
Container too ornate.
Top rose too high.
Right side too
straight.

SECOND PLACE WINNER
Score about 85.
Too broad above the roses.
Leaf rosette radiates
at the wrong
place.

MINIATURES IN COMPETITION

Top: **SECOND PLACE**
Score 90.
Container too small.

Top: **THIRD PLACE**
Score 80.
Too set in design.

Bottom: **FIRST PLACE**
Score 92.
Pleasing rhythm.
Lupine and
variegated oleander.

Bottom: **A LOSER**
Score 72.
Lacks grace.
Dry materials.
Fine container.

238

AN ASYMMETRICAL CENTERPIECE. It scores about 88 points. The hibiscus and caladium express delicacy and femininity. A higher leaf at right center would improve the design.

A SYMMETRICAL CENTERPIECE. It scores about 93 points. The lilies and loquat leaves suit the formal ultramodern design.

239

A WINNER that might score about 90 points. It expresses grace and serenity.

Index

Picture Index

of

Plant Materials

247

Flower arrangements. I've admired:

1-5-77. Corinthian Y.C. Perth. × ENS.

Table centerpieces, 12 × 14" ⟶ ◯

** Anemones - Red w. black center
Tulips - Yellow, Red w. White tips.
Daffodils - Yellow.
Daisies - White w. yellow centers.
Iris - forncan w. yellow (cecular line)

* Carnation · Bright pink & White

* Freesia - White & orange

Note: Filler - Eucolyptus & ferns.
      sparkling & cheerful for this time of year!

* Delicious fragrance
×× Anemones are what really tie it all together.